RAIDERS
FOREVER

RAIDERS FOREVER

Stars of the NFL's Most Colorful Team
Recall Their Glory Days

JOHN LOMBARDO

CB
CONTEMPORARY BOOKS

Library of Congress Cataloging-in-Publication Data

Lombardo, John.
    Raiders forever : stars of the NFL's most colorful team recall
their glory days / John Lombardo.
        p.   cm.
    Includes index.
    ISBN 0-658-00063-2
    1. Oakland Raiders (Football team)—History.   2. Football
players— United States—Interviews.   I. Title.
GV956.O24L64   2001
796.332'64'0979494—dc21   00-31408

Photos on pages xiv, 8, 22, 36, 48, 60, 70, 80, 90, 100, 110, 120, 128, 140, 152,
164, 176, 188, 202 copyright © Ron Riesterer, *Oakland Tribune*; pages 25, 53, 65,
75, 87, 93, 107, 160, 173, 179 courtesy of the author. Statistical information from
The Sporting News.

Cover and interior design by Nick Panos
Cover photograph copyright © Sports Illustrated

Published by Contemporary Books
A division of NTC/Contemporary Publishing Group, Inc.
4255 West Touhy Avenue, Lincolnwood (Chicago), Illinois 60712-1975 U.S.A.
Copyright © 2001 by John Lombardo
Printed in the United States of America
International Standard Book Number: 0-658-00063-2
        03 04 05 06 MV 19 18 17 16 15 14 13 12 11 10 9 8 7 6 5 4

Dedicated to Vincent Leo Lombardo
1927–1998

CONTENTS

ACKNOWLEDGMENTS

I owe a debt of gratitude to the former Oakland Raiders players who were willing to be interviewed to make this book a reality. Not all of their recollections are pleasant, yet they were willing to share both their successes and failures.

I'm particularly grateful to my agent Stephen Cogil Casari and his never-ending belief in the project. To the people at NTC/Contemporary Publishing, particularly Rob Taylor and Julia Anderson, thank you.

My gratitude also goes to Ken Samelson, to the research department at *The Sporting News*, to the NFL Hall of Fame, and to the folks in the Oakland Raiders organization who sent along useful information.

And much appreciation to my brother, Phil, and other family members who have encouraged and inspired me.

A note of special thanks to Megan, whose unwavering support is immensely appreciated.

INTRODUCTION

In sports, heroes are what we're after. Through them, we can chase our own failed dreams of glory, or maybe even relive the high school touchdown, the home run, or the game-winning jump shot at the buzzer.

But there's something else in sports that we love, secretly perhaps, more than our heroes—and that's the antihero. Everyone wears a tattoo, at least in his or her own mind.

Which is why the Oakland Raiders teams of the late 1960s through the 1970s still grab at us. The Raiders were a dynasty built by the myth of the antihero, a group defined by misfits, outlaws, and castoffs—a sort of halfway house for NFL players who had failed on other teams.

They were also a team built on the notion of the second chance, and the Raiders were the king of the scrap heap. Players like Ben Davidson, Ted Hendricks, and others were on their way out of the NFL, then landed in Oakland and found new life, joining a host of other players who prospered under owner Al Davis's "Just Win Baby" mantra.

Despite their outlaw reputation—and much of it was carefully cultivated by Davis—the Raiders found great success and triumph and celebrated with a swagger and style all their own, leaving the rest of the NFL to worry about rules. From the outside, hidden from the exploitative nature of professional football, the Raiders seemed to run counter to the grim business of the NFL. They broke curfew, drank, fought, slept around, and laughed at themselves and at the rest of the NFL, all the while winning in the last second.

And since the networks were smart enough to understand, the Raiders were usually the late game beamed back east as fall turned into dreary early winter. On those late, gloomy Sunday afternoons, those outlaw Raiders brought a lingering escape from the looming Monday-morning doom darkened by dead-end jobs, mortgages, bad marriages, false hopes, and fallen dreams.

But behind their well-chronicled exploits on and off the field, hard work and talent were just as much a part of the Raiders' success as the team's cultivated bad-boy reputation—heightened by their silver and black uniforms and eye-patched pirate logo. Not many teams practiced harder, and it showed.

Davis and the rest of the organization glowingly call themselves "The Team of the Decades," but really, the Raiders were the team of the 1970s. The 1960s were uneven years, filled with growing pains. The 1980s Raiders won a Super Bowl, but that decade's teams tried to live off faded glory and talent as Davis fled to Los Angeles. The 1990s were even worse, the team still searching for a part of its gloried past as if it could rekindle even just a smidgen of the same success.

Between 1967 and 1980, the Raiders averaged less than four losses a year and played in 11 league title games. Though plagued by postseason losses, the Raiders appeared in three Super Bowls, first with a loss after the 1967 season, then winning in Super Bowl XI after the 1976 season and Super Bowl XV after the 1980 season.

A generation may have passed since the Raiders ruled the NFL with their inimitable style, but the names still easily roll off our tongues. There's Ken Stabler, the hard-living quarterback whose blood ran cold on Sundays; Ted Hendricks, the oddest linebacker to ever ride a horse around a practice field; and Jack Tatum, the vicious safety whose head-hunting style put a New England Patriots receiver in a wheelchair for life. The Raiders had five Hall of Fame players on the team during that era in Jim Otto, Fred Biletnikoff, Gene Upshaw, Art Shell, and Hendricks, not to mention Davis, who despite a penchant for suing the NFL, was voted into the Hall of Fame in 1992.

Most of the former Raiders have managed to move on after football, but others, like John Matuszak and Lyle Alzado, couldn't make the transition. Alzado died in 1992 of brain cancer, his career a testament to the ravages of steroid abuse. Matuszak, one of the most popular Raiders to ever hit the bars in Jack London Square, died of an apparent heart attack in 1989. He was 38 years old.

We know their names and their reputations mostly from their play, but also because of a forced loyalty. Free agency in the 1970s NFL meant one thing: "You're cut."

And while today's liberal free agency structure in the NFL may have unchained the financial shackles from the players, it has also torn down much hope of any long-running dynasties. Today's Raiders still wear the same silver and black, but years of mediocrity have eroded the mystique.

But players from those great Raiders teams in the 1970s haven't faded away. They have aged, most now pushing 50; many are limping, some still unable to wean themselves off the warped life of NFL extremes. Yet they still capture our imagination, stirring not just dusty football memories but also sparking a certain spirit and image we would like to see in ourselves.

Flanked by JIM OTTO,
a young AL DAVIS
at the controls

1

THE EARLY DAYS

Gertrude Stein must have reached her famous "There is no there there" conclusion about Oakland by driving across the Bay Bridge into the city from San Francisco.

The double-decked bridge takes you over the San Francisco Bay, where off in the distance giant freighters circle, waiting to unload their cargo. Once you cross into the city, you're greeted by the gritty shipyards with railroad tracks protruding from the docks like spokes on a bicycle. Lining the railroad tracks are storage facilities, greasy spoons, cut-rate motels, and other staples of industrial Americana. Unlike its more stylish neighbor across the bay, Oakland is a working-class town, rough and tumble, with an underwhelming skyline and a distinctively low glamour quotient.

And when the Raiders were born, more by accident than by planning, no one could have predicted that the team and the city would perfectly complement each other—a bond shattered when Al Davis dumped Oakland for Los Angeles in 1982, only to return in 1995.

The Raiders first came to Oakland by way of Minneapolis, a city that was pegged as one of the original members of the American Football League when the league was created in August of 1959.

The AFL had already lined up investors in Minneapolis, but days before the deal was to be signed, NFL commissioner Pete Rozelle, fearful of the competition, promised the investors a more lucrative NFL franchise. No fools, the investors backed out of the upstart AFL, jumping at the chance to own a team in the established NFL—today's Minnesota Vikings.

The AFL, frozen out of Minnesota, turned to Oakland to appease Los Angeles Chargers owner Barron Hilton, who had threatened to leave the AFL if the league failed to put another team on the West Coast to create a rivalry.

Hilton's hardball tactics worked. The AFL investors, facing the desertion of one of the league's deep-pocketed owners, reluctantly gave a group of eight Oakland businessmen the league's final original franchise on January 30, 1960.

The early days were hardly prosperous. The Raiders' ticket office, according to former Raider great Ben Davidson, was a converted gas station and the team's offices were housed in three hotel rooms. The Raiders' team colors in those first few years were black and gold, a color scheme dictated not by some slick marketing campaign but by hand-me-down uniforms the Raiders inherited to save cash. Al Davis, then working as an assistant coach in San Diego, was nowhere in sight.

The Raiders' home games weren't even in Oakland until 1962, the team's third year of existence. The Raiders had been denied permission to play in Memorial Stadium in Berkeley and were forced to share Kezar Stadium in San Francisco with the NFL's 49ers, fueling Oakland's already decidedly stepsister reputation.

The Raiders lost their first game, against the Houston Oilers, by the score of 37–22 and finished their inaugural season with a 6–8 record while averaging a pitiful 9,612 fans per "home" game. The 1961 season proved even worse. The Raiders played in the newly built Candlestick Park in San Francisco and finished the season with a dismal 2–12 record as an average of 7,655 fans a game suffered through the horrendous season. The embarrassment continued in 1962, with the Raiders' sole victory coming in the last game of the season. The win ended the Raiders' losing streak at 19.

Then it all changed.

In 1963, the Raiders hired Davis as head coach, and one of the first moves he made was to change the uniform colors to silver and black.

The new color scheme gave the Raiders a new identity and they finished the season at 10–4, a remarkable retooling job by the team's 34-year-old head coach, who was named AFL Coach of the Year. All this from a frustrated athlete who never played a down of professional football.

Davis, a graduate of Erasmus High School in Brooklyn, began his coaching career after he graduated from Syracuse University, majoring in English. His first coaching job was as a line coach at Adelphi University, and his first head coaching job was for the U.S. Army, where he coached a team at Fort Belvoir, Virginia.

Davis's first taste of professional football came in the early 1950s, when the 24-year-old was an assistant for the Baltimore Colts. But it was back to the collegiate level in the mid-1950s, when Davis took the head coaching job at the Citadel and continued at the University of Southern California where he was an assistant.

When the AFL came to Los Angeles in 1960, Davis joined the Chargers staff as an offensive assistant. Ironically enough, he worked with Chuck Noll, who would later become Davis's fierce rival as coach of the Pittsburgh Steelers.

Davis's approach was to find talent where others saw failure.

It was Davis who took on Art Powell, a Canadian Football League star who married a white Canadian woman. Powell's reputation as a malcontent and his mixed marriage didn't sit well with many owners in 1963, but Davis had no qualms as long as Powell caught the ball. And Powell didn't disappoint. He was selected to play in the AFL All-Star Game in 1963, 1964, 1965, and 1966. He still holds the Raiders' single-game scoring records with 24 points, most touchdowns scored with six, and most receiving yards with 247. All three Raiders records were set by Powell on December 22, 1963, against the Houston Oilers.

"Davis looked at Powell and his wife and saw that while the skin didn't match, Art could catch a ball, so his thinking was that maybe we can forget about his wife's skin not matching," Ben Davidson said. "That was Al's first project."

That attitude played particularly well in the racially supercharged city where the Black Panther Party was rooted. Small-market Oakland and its fans began to take to the Raiders and their blue-collar style.

"People don't leave the East Coast to vacation in Oakland," said former Raiders running back Mark van Eeghen. "They go to San Francisco. Because of Oakland's image and the type of team image Al wanted to build, the bond was natural for us. When a game was over, we'd go down to Jack London Square to the same bars and restaurants as the fans. It was like a college atmosphere."

On their off days, many of the Raiders would take to the community, visiting local schools and hospitals like some oversized Boy Scout troop with hangovers.

"You'd go out someplace and people would break their arms to buy us dinner or a beer, and we would reciprocate in any way we could," said former Raiders great Jim Otto. "They'd have a family member who was sick and in the hospital and we'd get a phone call and we'd go over and see their sick and wounded. Then we'd go out and have a beer with them."

Davis left the Raiders in 1966 for a one-year tenure as AFL commissioner, and when he came back to Oakland, he began wheeling and dealing in earnest. He traded for cornerback Willie Brown, took a chance on veteran quarterback George Blanda, and drafted Gene Upshaw all in the same year. All would later be elected into the Pro Football Hall of Fame.

"Al and his staff would see that there was something left in an Art Powell or in a Ben Davidson if he was used the right way," Otto said. "Look at George Blanda. I mean, who wanted a 38-year-old quarterback who was having problems in Houston? How did we know that George had something left for the Raiders?"

Under head coach John Rauch, the Raiders went 13–1 in 1967 and beat the Houston Oilers for the right to play in Super Bowl II against the Green Bay Packers.

Though the Raiders were demolished by the Green Bay Packers, 33–14, the game served as a precursor to a decade of dominance.

From 1967 through 1969, the Raiders lost a total of four regular-season games in three seasons while winning 37 and playing to one tie. After the 1970 season when the Raiders lost to the Baltimore Colts in the AFC Championship game, the team appeared in a remarkable string of postseason play that ran from the 1972 through the 1977 seasons. During the Raiders run, the team played in five straight AFC championships from 1973 through 1977, and won the Super Bowl after the 1976 season. The team had 16 consecutive winning seasons from 1965 to 1980 and played in 18 postseason games.

Yet the impressive string of winning seasons couldn't shake the team's reputation for losing when it mattered most. Winning only one out of five AFC title games labeled the Raiders as choke artists, and the rate of failure still haunts the team.

Nevertheless, the team was fun to watch. The offense was wide open and vertical, the defense was vicious, and the team developed a knack for storming back in the final minutes, usually to pull out a win.

At the same time, the NFL was coming of age in the 1960s and early 1970s and the Raiders somehow seemed to be in the middle of it all. If there was controversy in the NFL, the Raiders seemed to be somehow involved.

There was the "Heidi Game" against the New York Jets in 1968 that forever changed how television viewed pro football. With 65 seconds the remaining and the Raiders down 32–29, NBC executives pulled the plug on the game to air the movie *Heidi*. How was the network to know that in the remaining minute the Raiders would march down the field and beat the Jets in what is now one of football's legendary games?

Then there was the "Immaculate Reception Game" against the Pittsburgh Steelers during the 1972 AFC playoffs that stunned a nationwide television audience after a Terry Bradshaw pass intended for Frenchy Fuqua bounced into the hands of Franco Harris just as Raiders safety Jack Tatum hit Fuqua in the back. Harris caught the ball just before it hit the Three Rivers Stadium turf and ran into the end zone. The officials huddled together for 10 minutes before ruling that the play stood, giving the Steelers a dramatic 13–7 win.

The loss still stings the Raiders organization today; there is no mention of the game in any official Raiders publications, including the media guide. It's as if Al Davis has ordered his public relations department to erase the game from the team's history books.

There were some dark moments to go along with the disappointment.

Safety George Atkinson's knockout blow of Steelers star receiver Lynn Swann in 1975 brought charges of dirty play and cheap hits into the limelight when Steelers coach Chuck Noll claimed the Raiders were full of the "criminal element." (Atkinson unsuccessfully sued Noll for libel and slander after the 1975 season.)

That image was solidified with fellow safety Jack Tatum's legal but devastating hit on New England Patriots receiver Darryl Stingley during a meaningless preseason game in 1978.

Still, it was the Raiders' Golden Age, led by Davis and a smart, young John Madden, who coached the team from 1970 to 1978.

As the wins added up, a mystique began to surround the team.

The NFL wasn't the slick, homogenized, multibillion-dollar enterprise that it is today. Under Davis's orders, the Raiders operated under a shroud of secrecy. Closed practices, little or no interest in public relations, and an annoying but effective policy of withholding roster cuts and waiver moves allowed Davis to gain a personnel edge that only heightened the mystery.

"People never knew what we were doing," Jim Otto said. "We locked up our training camps so nobody would see us practice. They never knew who was on waivers. Everything in those days was more secretive than today, where the NFL has all these bylaws that say you have to divulge all kinds of things at certain times and it has to be in the papers. We would divulge who our cuts were, but they were sent directly to the AFL office and the newspapers never got ahold of it."

Fueling the mystique was Davis himself. With his wide open, vertical offense, he was seen as an innovator who took chances on players other teams wouldn't touch. In the button-down NFL, Davis operated under two simple rules: be on time and win.

"Al is mysterious," said former Raider Pete Banaszak. "He treated us like he was the Messiah, so that's what we called him behind his back. But Al is really just a frustrated football player."

Off the field, Davis was fighting a legal battle in court to wrest control of the team from Raiders general partner Wayne Valley. In 1975, Davis assumed full control of the team, free to call all the shots.

But things started to unravel in 1978 as many of the Raiders stars began to fade. A burned-out Madden was in his final year, and the Raiders failed to make the playoffs for the first time in years. The team rebounded in 1980 under Madden's replacement, Tom Flores, by beating the Philadelphia Eagles, 27–10, in Super Bowl XV.

But it was the Raiders' last hurrah in Oakland. Davis successfully sued the NFL for antitrust violations, winning the right to move the team to Los Angeles but tearing out the heart of the team's image.

The 1982 Raiders were no longer from Oakland, and whatever magic the Raiders had created in the previous 22 years came to an abrupt end.

In 1984, the Los Angeles Raiders beat the Washington Redskins in Super Bowl XVIII, but it did nothing to win back betrayed fans in Oakland. After that, the Raiders began a steady fall from glory and Davis grew disenchanted in Los Angeles.

In 1995, Davis brought the Raiders back to Oakland, but the team's 12-year absence had caused irreparable harm to the sense of loyalty of many fans.

The Raiders haven't come close to duplicating their previous successes. The Raiders' struggle to sell out their home games, and the "Commitment to Excellence" slogan rings hollow around the league, given the Raiders' mediocre record in the past decade.

"The Raiders took the round peg and put it in the square hole," Ben Davidson said. "Al did it first, but other teams figured out that if a guy doesn't fit in he can still help. Al doesn't have the market cornered like he did early on."

Once again Davis is disenchanted in Oakland. He is suing city officials for what he claims is lost season-ticket revenue and he wants to make more money through the already overmarketed NFL, catering now to the well-heeled fan willing to shell out big dollars for club seats, personal seat licenses, and luxury suites— all designed to make owners even richer.

Raiders fans in Oakland haven't responded.

The city lacks a substantial corporate base to financially support the Raiders. Home games in the Coliseum don't sell out, causing the Raiders to black out local telecasts of their home games.

The fans, who've already been burned by Davis and face new threats that the team will relocate, have put even more distance between themselves and the great teams of the 1970s.

KEN STABLER takes aim.

2

THE SNAKE

Ken Stabler

Ken Stabler has been in Las Vegas for less than an hour on a still oven-hot Sunday night in the desert, and though he's spent the past six hours on an airplane, he keeps up his end of the deal we made to talk over drinks and dinner.

After weeks of phone calls and canceled plans, Stabler's secretary finally found a hole in his schedule and arranged for us to meet in Vegas, where Stabler was to spend three days glad-handing tobacco merchants as part of his promotional deal with Swisher Cigars.

After I reached Stabler by phone at his hotel, he wearily suggested we meet in a bar just off the lobby of the fabled Las Vegas Hilton. Fifteen minutes after our appointed meeting time, he strolled into the lobby dressed for some action in a well-cut dark green suit and a starched pin-striped dress shirt with monogrammed cuffs.

There's a slight limp to Stabler's gait, and his face is weathered by thousands of last-call nights, but it's his shock of thin white hair that dominates his appearance, making him seem a bit older than 53. He still wears his hair long, just as he did in his playing days when it flowed out the back of his helmet, a perfect example of the message of fuck-you Raiders independence sent to the rest of the then-conservative NFL.

One of the first things you notice about Stabler is that he's bigger than you'd think.

Then again, NFL quarterbacks are always much bigger in person, because on television, the massive linemen tend to distort the still-oversize dimensions of skill players like quarterbacks and running backs.

Stabler wears both his Super Bowl ring and the ring he earned by leading Alabama to an undefeated season and the national championship in 1966. He usually keeps the gaudy, diamond-studded Super Bowl ring safe at home, but the Swisher executives pay him good coin to talk about the old days while sporting the crown jewel of his career—it gives them something to talk about back at the office.

After a handshake and a quick introduction, Stabler displays some of his native Alabama hospitality with a sharp clink of his glass against my beer bottle and a toast to our meeting. Though we just met minutes before, Stabler acts as if you are one of his best friends sitting on his porch back home in Mobile, killing a hot summer night over cocktails. His voice is thick with a south Alabama drawl, but there is a cool, flat tone in his speech that makes him sound like an airline pilot calmly explaining that the violent yawing of the airplane 35,000 feet over the ocean is nothing but a bit of light chop.

No wonder his linemen would have just as soon die as allow a sack.

Stabler's drink of choice is Southern Comfort on the rocks, a nod to one of his former promotional deals with the whiskey maker. Over the first drink, he tells me the plan: we are to meet his agent and his marketing assistant, then head to dinner. Only there's some confusion over where they are to meet us, so Stabler and I start talking not about his Raiders career but his days as a star pitcher back at Foley High School in southern Alabama. The stringbean lefty was a strikeout artist who ended up being drafted by the New York Yankees.

"Really, I was a better pitcher than quarterback," he says. "I was real skinny and I could throw. I used to match up against [300-game winner and major league baseball Hall of Famer] Don Sutton, and I gave him his only loss in his high school career by beating him 1–0. The Yankees were going to give me a college education and $30,000, but at Alabama, there was the opportunity to play for Coach Bryant."

And in the early 1960s, there was no place for an Alabama high school football star to consider other than the University of

Alabama—unless, of course, you were a black high school super-star and never got recruited.

But Stabler was white, and better yet, had been a star at Foley High, where in three varsity seasons he helped his team to a 29–1 record. Though his senior class graduated just 47 students, the football team captured three state championships, with Stabler starring as a quarterback and defensive back.

Stabler was a high school all-everything and a standout in the statewide all-star games.

Auburn University recruited him hard, but after the legendary Bryant paid a visit to the Stabler living room, there was no doubt where Stabler was headed.

"Alabama football is embedded in our culture," Stabler said while ordering another round.

But after draining his second Southern Comfort, he's getting antsy.

The bar's too bright, the crowd's too dull, and the night is too fresh. The bar is the type of establishment that provides far too little cover, and it is exactly the kind of place that spelled trouble for Stabler and his Raider running mates during their playing days. Even now, there's the sense that he's being watched too closely, so after his agent and marketing assistant finally join us at the bar, the four of us bolt for what Stabler says is a nice little spot some-where else.

Since Stabler is the quarterback, you tend to instinctively follow his lead, and after a serpentine walk through the casino, past a statue of Elvis Presley (who'd holed up at the Hilton when he played Vegas, and it seems oddly right that the man with a former rock and roll lifestyle lead us past the shrine to the King), and down a dark hallway, he suddenly stops and opens an unmarked black door that appears to be the entrance to a service closet.

Except it's no closet, it's the back door to a lounge where at the moment a woman in a slinky dress is on stage, deep into a badly produced Michael Jackson medley.

Stabler makes a beeline to the back bar and high-fives the bar-tender he remembers from a few years before when he worked for the Hilton as a casino promoter. A quick signal by the bartender sends a waitress to lead us to a dark table in the back of the room, where a round of drinks and a tab have already been set up.

"I never walk through the front door of a place if I can help it," Stabler says, and immediately his nickname of "The Snake" begins to make a whole lot of sense.

It's now apparent that the drinks will serve as dinner, so we all order another round, with Stabler controlling the action.

"This all right?" he asks as he begins to snap his fingers to the music. At the moment the singer is imploring the crowd that if we want to make the world a better place, we have to take a look at ourselves in the mirror. It's an absolutely perfect bit of lounge-act Vegas, thoroughly compelling in its tackiness yet somehow enjoyable at the same time.

But it's not Michael Jackson that Stabler wants to talk about. It's Bear Bryant.

Inside Stabler's billfold is a faded red Alabama crescent that he shows off as readily as his Super Bowl ring. It's an indication of his allegiance to the school, where he still has ties to the football program as a radio color announcer during the season.

He was Bear Bryant material from the get-go, a hard-drinking southern boy with a taste for fast cars and women who was smart enough and tough enough to satisfy the crafty old coach.

"You are so young when you play there that you don't even begin to understand what you are being a part of," Stabler said. "At the time, Alabama had won 12 national championships. But when you are 18 years old, you don't realize what you are around and what Coach Bryant stood for."

Since freshmen were prohibited from playing on the varsity team, Stabler spent his freshman year mainly getting used to the Alabama offense, a basic offense that had the quarterbacks call their own plays. It would be good training for the Raiders offense, where Stabler called his own game and became the master of improvisation.

Even if the NCAA had not prohibited freshmen from playing on the varsity, Stabler wouldn't have played a down, because in 1964, Joe Namath was the team's firmly established quarterback. Then Steve Sloan took over with Namath's departure, leading the Crimson Tide to a 9–1–1 record and a national championship with Stabler as the backup.

The following year as a starter, Stabler picked up right where Sloan had left off. The Tide went undefeated and thrashed Nebraska, 34–7, in the 1967 Sugar Bowl, only to have the national championship go to Notre Dame.

For Stabler, it was a coming-out party of sorts, as he threw for nearly 1,000 yards and set a Southeastern Conference passing record with a remarkable 65 percent completion rate. He also rushed for 397 yards.

He grew to respect Bryant, finally understanding what it was like to play for a legend.

"The reason we won was because of him," Stabler said. "He would always say, 'I'll take mine and beat yours, or I'll take yours, and beat mine.' "

Cementing the relationship was Bryant's routine of taking the quarterbacks for a walk after the pregame meal served at the downtown Birmingham hotel where the team stayed before home games.

Strolling around the block in his houndstooth hat and plaid blazer while smoking nonfiltered Chesterfields, Bryant would quiz Stabler and the other quarterbacks on specific game situations to prepare for on the field that afternoon. Bryant would sidle up to the quarterbacks and, while spitting out the tobacco from his Chesterfields, pepper his players to make sure they were ready.

"He'd ask questions like what if the game was tied and we had to go for the two-point conversion, and I'd say that I would roll out and give myself some kind of options," Stabler said, knowing what satisfied the old coach. "During that walk, he'd always say that as quarterbacks, we were his personal representatives on the field. It made you figure out who you were, walking in all those footsteps of other quarterbacks."

But as Ken was winning games for Bryant, it was hardly a happy time for the Stabler family.

Back home in Foley, Stabler's father Leroy, or "Slim," was drinking harder than ever and becoming increasingly frustrated. Whether it was Slim's World War II battle fatigue, or the frustrations of raising a family on a car mechanic's wages, Slim Stabler was a difficult man to live with.

He pushed Ken, sometimes embarrassing him publicly after a few too many bourbons. As Ken got older and his stardom brought him more attention and more money, Slim grew meaner.

"Those are not good memories at all," Ken said. "We had a real adversarial relationship. Because I was making money, he held that against me, and I didn't like the way he treated my mother. He was uneducated and had demons inside. When he was in the war, he didn't peel potatoes, he killed people."

It was Ken's mother Sally who managed to keep the Stabler family together, though it sometimes came with a price.

"My dad was 6-foot-6 and went 230 pounds, and when I was 18, I had to keep him from killing my sister Carolyn and my mother. What my father put her through—well, perseverance is what comes to mind, and that's what she taught me," Stabler said.

This is about as much as he wants to talk about his childhood, and any related questions are put off by a steady stream of cigar-smoking, mostly middle-aged guys who have noticed Stabler despite the bar's dark cover. Stabler seamlessly interrupts our conversation to say hello, shake hands, and sign autographs and then immediately picks up our conversation at the exact point he left off.

Meantime, the drinks keep coming and so do the memories.

As the Raiders' second-round pick in 1968, Stabler was drafted behind another quarterback named Eldridge Dickey, a black quarterback out of Tennessee State. Negotiation was hardly an issue for Stabler—he took what the Raiders offered, even though he was also drawing interest from major league baseball teams despite the fact that he didn't pitch in his final two years at Alabama.

"I signed a four-year deal with the Raiders for $16,000, $18,000, $20,000, and $22,000, with a signing bonus of $50,000 for a total package of $125,000, and I was happy to have it," Stabler said. "Money was never an issue when we played. We played hung over, we played with wife problems, and we played with drug problems, but at one o'clock Sunday afternoon we had to put it all aside and go win for each other and for John [Madden]. The money came as we won, but the most I ever made was $500,000 a year. Today, I'd be making around $6 million, but that's what television has done to the game."

Stabler's professional career was nearly over before it began.

He didn't have a strong enough arm to handle the Raiders' vertical passing game, and his knee was still injured when he reported to training camp in the summer of 1968, the year after the Raiders lost to the Green Bay Packers in Super Bowl II with rifle-armed Daryle Lamonica firmly entrenched as the Raiders' quarterback.

Stabler's rookie year was a wash, as the Raiders shuffled him off to the Spokane Shockers of the Continental League, where he played just one game, completing just 17 of 41 passes, with three interceptions. It was an awful debut, and the Raiders brought Stabler back to Oakland, where he sat idle on the injured reserve squad. It was a lackluster beginning to his career, and things didn't improve much until 1972, when he saw some significant playing time and began to display his strengths, including his touch and his innate ability read a defense and make quick decisions.

Before each game, Stabler met with his offensive line to discuss what plays would work in various situations. It not only helped him gain a greater understanding of the opposing team, it built a critical sense of trust between the then-quarterback and his linemen.

And what Stabler lacked in arm strength, he made up for with an uncanny knack for finding the open receiver. While he bided his time on the bench, he listened and learned from George Blanda, the tough and timeless quarterback who took Stabler under his wing and taught him how to think on a football field.

"I couldn't bust an egg, but I was real accurate," Stabler said. "Because I didn't have the strong arm, I had to get away with thinking a little more. I'd use Freddy [Biletnikoff] here, and I'd find Cliff Branch there, and then I'd use [Dave] Casper when I had to."

Finally, the Raiders' investment in Stabler began to pay off in the middle of 1973 when he beat out Lamonica and became the Raiders' starting quarterback.

With Stabler at the helm, the Raiders went 9–4–1, losing to the Miami Dolphins 27–10, in the AFC championship game. It was the start of five consecutive seasons in which the Raiders reached the AFC title game, leading to a Super Bowl win over the Vikings in 1976. There should have been more Super Bowls, only the Raiders couldn't find a way to beat the Pittsburgh Steelers more than once in postseason play.

"We dominated the AFC West for 10 years, and we were better on offense than they were and they were better on defense than we were," Stabler said.

During the decade, Stabler piled up big numbers, making All-Pro in 1973, 1974, 1976, and 1977, and the Raiders record book is littered with his name. He holds the single-season marks for most passes attempted at 325, most completions at 188, and most yards gained passing at 2,398. His single-game records include best completion rate of 82 percent, which he set on December 22, 1973, against the Pittsburgh Steelers. In his 15-year career, Stabler completed 2,270 passes for 27,938 yards and 194 touchdowns.

What's not listed in the Raiders' record book is his serene presence on the field, a characteristic that not only won him the respect of his teammates but made him the master of come-from-behind victories.

While Madden would rant and rave on the sidelines, Stabler would saunter over during a time-out with the game on the line, push his helmet up so the face mask would rest atop his head, and calm Madden down.

"John was kind of like an unmade bed," Stabler said. "So I seemed real cool compared to him, but I don't really know where it comes from."

Stabler's innate feel for the game allowed him to improvise on the run, and while he never obeyed a bed check in his life, he never screwed around on the field, displaying total command in the huddle.

"I ran a real serious huddle, and nobody talked but me," he said. "My huddle was no place for chatter. There was too much money on the line. Everyone in that huddle was bigger than me, but you call a play and you can take them from a two-car garage to a three-car garage. That was always the perspective I had. Move the chains, score points, and everyone will follow you. There were all kinds of intangibles, but I've always had the ability to make people better."

Nowhere was that philosophy more apparent than in the Raiders' Super Bowl XI win over the Minnesota Vikings, where Stabler calmly completed 12 of 19 passes for 180 yards with no interceptions. More important than the numbers was his play calling; four big passes to Fred Biletnikoff on separate possessions put the Raiders inside the Minnesota Vikings five-yard line and helped make Biletnikoff the game's Most Valuable Player.

Then there was the Raiders' 1977 double-overtime playoff game against the Baltimore Colts, a game in which Stabler completed 21 passes, including three touchdown passes to Dave Casper, to beat the Colts, 37–31, in a wild shoot-out of a game that had Stabler improvising plays all over Baltimore's Memorial Stadium.

But it wasn't his remarkable statistics that defined Stabler that day. It was his absolute calmness, which stunned even Madden, who had grown accustomed to Stabler's serenity as all hell broke loose around him.

During a time-out late in the sudden-death period, Stabler walked over to Madden, who was storming on the sidelines, screaming at his quarterback over the din of 60,000 Baltimore fans.

"It was during the sixth period," Madden said, "and we had the ball in scoring range when I called time out. Ken came over and had his helmet tilted on the back of his head and I was carrying on and blubbering, and he says to me, 'You know what, John?' and I'm thinking he's going to suggest a play and I said, 'What, Kenny?' He said, 'These fans are sure getting their money's worth' and then he goes back out on the field and throws a touchdown pass to Casper. He never let my excitement affect him. He probably tuned me out."

The thrill of the Raiders' double-overtime win over the Colts was short-lived, however, as Stabler and Co. lost in the AFC championship game to the Denver Broncos the following weekend.

Stabler didn't know it at the time, but it was the beginning of the end of his Raiders career.

The following season, the Raiders went 9–7, missing the play-offs for the first time since 1971. Stabler's completion rate hovered at a respectable 58 percent, but he threw 30 interceptions, 10 more than in 1977.

As the interceptions mounted, so did the pressure on him, and soon enough, he and owner Al Davis took turns criticizing each other through the media.

In 1979, the Raiders were an old team, and when Stabler reported late to training camp, the rift with Davis began growing larger by the week. The Raiders finished the season with a 9–7 record, again missing the playoffs, but the team's disappointing performance didn't affect Stabler's numbers, as he threw for 3,615 yards with a completion rate of 61 percent. He also threw for 26 touchdowns, and his interceptions fell to 22.

But Stabler's relationship with Davis had been damaged beyond repair, and before the 1980 season, he was traded to the Houston Oilers for Dan Pastorini.

"Al had said something about me and related me to a 20-game baseball pitcher going 10–10, and then I said that the first place you should look at when things are going wrong is at the top. He took a swing at me and I swung back, and the next thing I knew I was getting my mail in Houston."

It was a sudden ending to Stabler's remarkable Raiders career, and it represented the end of the Raiders' glory years that had brought both delight and frustration to Oakland fans, as the Raiders could get to the Super Bowl only once during their decade of domination.

Though Stabler played two seasons in Houston and three more for the New Orleans Saints before he retired in 1984, he was never anything but a Raider.

The organization was a perfect fit for his undisciplined style and personality. All he had to do was show up and play.

"John just let us go," Stabler said. "From our end, we understood that the reason we didn't have curfew was because we won. If we lost every fucking Sunday, there damn sure would have been a curfew, but there were no problems when we won. The problems came when we lost, and I don't remember losing much."

Even training camp, which in those days lasted two months, never bothered Stabler. He put his work in and then he'd roam the Santa Rosa bars at night. On occasion, he'd broker a deal with Madden for the players to have a morning off so they could nurse their hangovers after a night of revelry to break the monotony of camp.

"I couldn't wait to get to Santa Rosa to see the guys. I couldn't wait to get to training camp and go out every night and shake dice for drinks," Stabler said.

When Stabler retired as a battered 38-year-old in 1984, there wasn't anything that he could find that could come close to the feeling he got on the field.

Back home in Alabama, he struggled to make the adjustment to a life outside of football. In between charity golf events, Stabler dabbled in real estate and other ventures, none of which proved satisfying or profitable.

"There is very little crowd noise when you sell a piece of real estate," he said. "It was hard to find the same gratification of what you get when you throw a touchdown pass. As a player, you go through so many things together. We had so many ups and downs. You knew you were going to get hurt and you knew you were going to get the glory, and there are all types of emotions you go through."

After a few years of scuffling, Stabler went back to doing what he does best: being Ken Stabler, NFL legend.

Stabler realized that instead of trying to replace his football identity, he'd cash in on it—and it has worked.

Running his business out of Mobile, Stabler flies around the country making personal appearances, meeting speaking engagements, and flacking for companies looking to use his fame to entertain clients and customers. His own website is under construction, and there's a plan to convert Stabler's house in the historic slave district in Mobile into a cigar and piano bar. He wants to call it Snake's Place.

As long as people remember the Raiders, Stabler has a commodity to sell. But despite the ability to make a good living off his long-ago career, there are regrets.

Back in his scuffling days, he wrote a book that revealed too much about the Raiders' hard-living lifestyle, alienating himself from some of his former teammates. Then there are the battles he fought in public with Al Davis that prematurely ended his career.

"I should have kept my mouth shut and kept playing for the Raiders," Stabler said.

Now married to his third wife, Molly, and the father of two daughters, Stabler, who has another child from a previous marriage, looks at his career from a different perspective. He wants to secure his place in the league by becoming a member of the Pro Football Hall of Fame.

Stabler's been eligible since 1989, but he knows it's a long shot considering that he played in only one Super Bowl, while contemporaries of his, people like Terry Bradshaw and Bob Griese, made multiple appearances in the big game.

"They got more jewelry, but I have better numbers," Stabler said as the night dragged on, twisted by too many drinks and a suddenly oppressive nightclub haze.

It's a line that he undoubtedly will use in about eight hours when he resurrects his glory days on command for dozens of cigar salesmen at a Vegas trade show.

Ken Michael Stabler

Born December 25, 1945, at Holey, AL
Height: 6'3" Weight: 210
High School: Foley, AL.
Received degree in physical education from University of Alabama.

Named AFC Player of the Year by *The Sporting News*, 1974 and 1976.
Named to *The Sporting News* AFC All-Star Team, 1974 and 1976.
Led NFL in passing with 103.7 points in 1976.
Selected by Oakland AFL in 2nd round (52nd player selected) of 1968 AFL–NFL draft.
Member of Oakland Raiders' taxi squad, 1968.
Did not play in 1969.
Traded by Oakland Raiders to Houston Oilers for quarterback Dan Pastorini, March 17, 1980.
Released by Houston Oilers, July 15, 1982; signed as free agent by New Orleans Saints, August 24, 1982.
Retired, October 26, 1984.
Played in Continental Football League with Spokane Shockers, 1968.
Selected by New York Yankees organization in 10th round of free-agent draft, June 13, 1966.

				PASSING							RUSHING				TOTAL	
Year	Club	G.	Att.	Cmp.	Pct.	Gain	T.P.	P.I.	Avg.	Att.	Yds.	Avg.	TD.	TD.	Pts.	F.
1968	Spokane CoFL	1	41	17	34.1	125	0	3	3.05	None				0	0	—
1970	Oakland NFL	3	7	2	28.6	52	0	1	7.43	7	−4	−4.0	0	0	0	1
1971	Oakland NFL	14	48	24	50.0	268	1	4	5.58	4	29	7.3	2	2	12	1
1972	Oakland NFL	14	74	44	59.5	524	4	3	7.08	6	27	4.5	0	0	0	2
1973	Oakland NFL	14	260	163	*62.7	1997	14	10	7.68	21	101	4.8	0	0	0	5
1974	Oakland NFL	14	310	178	57.4	2469	*26	12	7.96	12	−2	−0.2	1	1	6	3
1975	Oakland NFL	14	293	171	58.4	2296	16	24	7.84	6	−5	−0.8	0	0	0	4
1976	Oakland NFL	12	291	194	*66.7	2737	27	17	*9.41	7	−2	−0.3	1	1	6	5
1977	Oakland NFL	13	294	169	57.5	2176	20	20	7.40	3	−3	−1.0	0	0	0	3
1978	Oakland NFL	16	406	237	58.4	2944	16	30	7.25	4	0	0.0	0	0	0	9
1979	Oakland NFL	16	498	304	61.0	3615	26	22	7.26	16	−4	−0.3	0	0	0	10
1980	Houston NFL	16	457	293	64.1	3202	13	28	7.01	15	−22	−1.5	0	0	0	7
1981	Houston NFL	13	285	165	57.9	1988	14	18	6.98	10	−3	−0.3	0	0	0	7
1982	New Orleans NFL	8	189	117	61.9	1343	6	10	7.11	3	−4	−1.3	0	0	0	4
1983	New Orleans NFL	14	311	176	56.6	1988	9	18	6.39	9	−14	−1.6	0	0	0	4
1984	New Orleans NFL	3	70	33	47.1	339	2	5	4.84	1	−1	−1.0	0	0	0	1
	Pro Totals—15 years	184	3793	2270	59.8	27938	194	222	7.37	118	93	0.8	4	4	24	66

Quarterback Rating Points: 1970 (18.5), 1971 (39.4), 1972 (95.8), 1973 (88.5), 1974 (94.8), 1975 (67.6), 1976 (103.7), 1977 (75.2), 1978 (63.1), 1979 (82.2), 1980 (68.6), 1981 (69.5), 1982 (71.9), 1983 (61.4), 1984 (41.3). Total—75.1.

Additional pro statistics: Recovered one fumble and fumbled once for minus 10 yards, 1971; recovered two fumbles, 1972, 1975, 1980, and 1981; recovered one fumble and fumbled five times for minus one yard, 1973; recovered one fumble, 1976; fumbled three times for minus three yards, 1977; recovered one fumble and fumbled nine times for minus four yards, 1978; recovered five fumbles and fumbled 10 times for minus 30 yards, 1979; fumbled seven times for minus 16 yards, 1980; fumbled seven times for minus 13 yards, 1981.
    Played in AFC Championship Game following 1973 through 1977 seasons.
    Played in NFL Championship Game following 1976 season.
    Played in Pro Bowl following 1973, 1974, and 1977 seasons.

ART SHELL (78) in a familiar position—next to linemate GENE UPSHAW

3

ART SHELL

Art Shell is a football coach, and that means when he says to meet him at 2:00 P.M., you make damn sure you're there at least 15 minutes early.

Punctuality is the first rule of thumb for every football coach, and after spending almost two decades coaching in the NFL, Shell first and foremost wants people to be on time.

That's why I spent a half hour in a McDonald's restaurant that sits on a hill above the Atlanta Falcons' practice facility in Suwanee, Georgia, killing time before I was to meet Shell, who had just returned from a weeklong vacation on the West Coast.

On that rare week off, Shell and his wife, Janice, took a leisurely train ride up the coast from Los Angeles to Seattle, where they visited his friend and former teammate Otis Sistrunk, who never attended college so the team's beat writers claimed he went to the University of Mars.

Though Shell and Sistrunk are friends, there is one major difference between the two former Raiders: never in a million years would anyone claim Shell was from the University of Mars. He wouldn't even tell you he graduated from what was then Maryland State College and is now University of Maryland–Eastern Shore unless you had a good reason to ask. Nor would he tell you that after his mom died when he was 15, he grew up quick helping his father, Art Sr., with household chores and getting his three younger brothers and one sister ready for school.

"Mom passed away when I was a sophomore, and I went to school playing football and basketball. My dad raised all of us. It was a challenge, but he took it upon himself and didn't want to bring anyone into the family atmosphere who would disrupt anything," is about all Shell says about his high school years.

We are talking in his bunkerlike office tucked deep inside the Falcons' complex. Outside the temperature is a sweltering 101 degrees, but inside, it's an icebox, with the air-conditioning cranked up not only to fight off Georgia's sultry July heat but probably to keep the coaches from falling asleep on their desks after spending hours on end watching film and figuring out how to return to the Super Bowl.

Shell's office is spartan. There is a small picture of Janice on his desk and one of those small plaques you find in a Hallmark store that have typically insipid inspirational messages like "Tomorrow Is the First Day of the Rest of Your Life" or "Life Is Not a Dress Rehearsal" stenciled onto them.

Shell's plaque reads:

To achieve all that's possible
We must attempt the impossible
To be as much as we can be
We must dream of being more.

Though Shell would never say it, he tries to abide by the plaque's basic tenet, and who knows, maybe it helped him develop into one of the proudest, most consistent, and most courteous offensive tackles ever to crush the bejesus out of just about every defensive tackle lined up against the Hall of Famer during his 15-year career.

Today, as offensive line coach for the Falcons, Shell keeps alive his goal of getting another crack as an NFL head coach. He was the league's first black head coach in the NFL's modern era when Al Davis hired him to replace Mike Shanahan in 1989. Shell was the Raiders' head coach until 1994, when Davis fired him and hired Mike White. But Shell certainly looks the part in his khaki pants, gray golf shirt with the red Falcons logo embroidered on the

Shell: yesterday's All-Pro lineman is today's NFL *coach.*

right chest pocket, and a pristine pair of white running shoes that look fresh out of the box.

Shell was born in 1946, but he looks ten years younger.

He has an open, friendly face and his full head of hair shows no sign of gray. Though he stands 6 feet 5 inches and weighs at least 250 pounds, he has a lightness about him. Unlike so many big men, Shell doesn't lumber when he walks. Instead, his gait is smooth and seemingly unaffected by his 15 years spent in the trenches.

Despite his massive size, Shell has a gentle presence about him. He speaks softly, yet he commands your immediate attention by his quiet demeanor.

As a player, he was known as being unfailingly polite on the football field. He never spent time working up a false hatred for an opposing player, a common psychological ploy used by other players to help justify spending a Sunday afternoon trying to hurt the guy across the line of scrimmage.

In lieu of hate, Shell would develop an inflated sense of respect for whomever he would have to block on game day. Didn't matter if the guy was a rookie or a washed-up veteran—come Sunday, Shell would be playing against the best defensive lineman in the history of the NFL, at least in his own mind.

"By game time, the guy I played against was a world-beater, the best to play his position. I'd compare notes with Gene Upshaw and he'd say, 'Art, what the hell are you talking about, your guy is a stiff.' But I did respect my opponents, and I loved to greet them on the field. If they came close to sacking the quarterback, I'd say, 'Oh, that was close, that was a good pass rush.' I'd give 'em a little sugar."

Shell's demeanor confounded his coaches, who had a hard time understanding why such a big man could be so kind on the football field.

"I always felt that you didn't have to hate each other on the field. From high school to the pros, I always heard that I wasn't mean enough, but I sincerely mean it that you don't have to be angry to play football. It is a job, and you treat it as such. I think that during the course of my 15-year career, I was angry three times about something that someone on the other team did to me."

Shell's measured approach to his opponent masked his intensity to succeed. He absolutely hated to give up a sack. To Shell, allowing his man to get to quarterback Ken Stabler was a personal affront, a breakdown of the worst kind.

It didn't happen often.

Besides having tremendous natural strength, Shell had quick, nimble feet that belied his bulk, allowing him to backpedal and adjust to the oncoming pass rusher.

Playing at such a small, unknown school like Maryland State–Eastern Shore College didn't provide Shell the chance to develop the best blocking techniques, but he also played college basketball, which allowed him to develop an astounding athleticism.

He became an absolute steamroller of a lineman, with the feet of a wide receiver. The combination of his size and nimbleness of foot provided the perfect ingredients to enable him to dominate a line of scrimmage. Not only could he blast holes open, but those quick feet allowed him to keep himself between the quarterback and the pass rusher.

"I was a power guy in the running game and I had enough finesse for pass protection. But when I would play basketball, I always tried to find the smallest guy to guard, because he'd make me move. I always felt that basketball would carry over and help me play football."

Shell was such a good basketball player that the president of Maryland State–Eastern Shore ordered him back on the basketball team when he discovered that Shell had left the team after a new coach took over.

"He called and asked why I wasn't playing, and I said the new coach wanted his own people in there, but the university president told me to get back on the team. So I went back and played the second half of my senior season," Shell said, laughing for the first time since we began talking.

Maryland State–Eastern Shore was hardly a powerhouse football program, and the school was lucky to land Shell, who was an All-State basketball and football player at Bonds–Wilson High in Charleston, South Carolina.

After he graduated, Shell was packed and ready to board a bus to play for Eddie Robinson at Grambling when Maryland State–Eastern Shore football coach Roosevelt Gilliam paid a visit.

"I had my ticket and everything ready to go to Grambling," Shell said. "But [Gilliam] came down from Maryland and picked me up. He said he wasn't leaving until I agreed to go with him. He took my dad aside and promised him I would get an education."

That was all Art Shell Sr., who never made it to high school, needed to hear. Soon Art Jr. was on his way north to Maryland and to a future he could only dream about.

He played center his first two years in college, then switched to tackle and was named Little All-America offensive tackle in his senior year. "I took the offer to Maryland State because I had heard about [players] like Roger Brown and Johnny Samples who went to the school. I became a starter, and I also played defensive tackle, because we all played both ways back then," said Shell.

Soon enough, the questionnaires from NFL teams began arriving in the mail.

That's how NFL coaches scouted back in those days. They'd ask about size, speed, and position, and you'd send it back. Contact was minimal until draft day, when the school's athletic director dragged you out of class to tell you that you were picked.

When a questionnaire came from the Raiders, Shell dutifully filled it out and then figured that he would be drafted by the San Diego Chargers.

"I drew interest from a lot of teams, and I really thought I'd go to San Diego. All I got from the Raiders was a questionnaire. But the Raiders drafted me in the third round in 1968. As I understand it now, the Raiders missed out the year before on drafting [Kansas City Chief linebacker] Willie Lanier, who had played at a historically black small school, and they vowed that if a talented small-school player was available, they weren't going to miss out on him. But back then, what got my attention about the Raiders was watching their games on television and seeing Jim Otto snap the ball without looking."

Soon enough, Shell would be on the same field with Otto, though he didn't win a starting job with the Raiders until his third season. He was raw, a mountain of potential who needed time to learn the proper techniques that he had missed in college.

"Being from a small school, I never really had individual coaching, and I needed to develop my technique. But the Raiders were patient with me. It was a big change going to the Raiders from a small black school."

Though Shell needed work, Davis and John Madden saw the potential and liked his attitude.

"I felt like a Raider from day one. If you came in the door and weren't a big-mouth rookie, they took care of you. But if you were a smart-ass, they made it difficult. I kept my eyes and ears open and kept my mouth shut, and the coaches made me feel comfortable. Coming in, I knew they had a tradition of winning. I understood the history of Al Davis and how they took off and started winning. I understood they were a high-powered offense and believed in gang-tackling and playing tough physical football."

Shell finally cracked the Raiders' starting lineup in 1971, and he never left it until he retired in 1982.

"The coaches told me that if I didn't win a starting job within three years, I should quit," Shell said.

Instead of quitting, Shell began a string of 207 league games, ranking him third in Raiders history behind center Jim Otto and guard Gene Upshaw in that category.

Offensive linemen work in relative anonymity, but Shell's peers knew his talent. They voted him to play in eight Pro Bowls, the most of any Raider from that era.

Shell, along with Upshaw, owned the left offensive side of the line of scrimmage against their opponents. The two linemen, both from small towns and from small colleges, were radically different. Shell was as quiet as Upshaw was brash, but they played together for so long and so well that each knew what the other was thinking.

Put them both in a room today and it's likely that Shell would stand to Upshaw's left, where he lined up for 12 years.

"We clicked because of the total respect we had for each other," Shell said. "I could say things to him that he wouldn't accept from anybody else. I could chew him out and vice versa. But we could make adjustments just before the ball was snapped. I knew how he'd react without saying a word."

Both grew to have such a grasp of the game that Ken Stabler would amble over to them before a game and ask both what particular plays would work. More often than not, when there was a critical first down to be had, they'd call their own numbers, with help from tight end Dave Casper. In the Raiders' playbook, that was known as the "bob trio." On the field, it usually came in a critical first-down situation.

"If you'd look at us in the huddle, you'd always see Gene with his head between his legs, looking back at the defense, and I'd be standing with my head half turned toward the line of scrimmage. We always tried to find out what we had to do, and Snake would always come to us and ask us how we wanted to work."

Though Upshaw was the talker, other players would come to Shell in the huddle, knowing that when Shell had something to say, Stabler would listen.

"When Snake walked into the huddle, it was his, but if I had something to say, I'd catch him before the huddle. I used to be the carrier pigeon for Cliff Branch. Cliff would insist he was open and could go deep, so I'd talk to Snake about it and he'd tell me that Cliff thought he was open but he didn't see the safety rotating back. So I go to Cliff and tell him that he didn't see the safety rotating back, but it got to the point where Cliff was always open."

Shell set higher standards for himself as his career progressed, refusing to believe that as a perennial Pro Bowler, he was the best tackle in the NFL. To Shell, there was no such thing as a perfectly played game. It simply couldn't exist.

"If I played against great players, then I felt I needed to get a stalemate and then we could win. But I could tell you my flaws in a game before we even got to the locker room. I never wanted my guy even to get close to the quarterback. I could always find ways that I screwed up."

There was one game that even Shell might admit he played without fault—Super Bowl XI—a performance that may stand as one of the finest ever by an offensive lineman.

On that ninth day of January 1977, in front of more than 100,000 fans in the Rose Bowl, Shell's assignment was Jim Marshall, one of the leaders of the Minnesota Vikings' famed front defensive line known as the Purple People Eaters.

"I remember looking down at the Vikings during warm-ups and the defensive linemen were warming up without pads, acting like it was going to be a walk in the park. I took Gene [Upshaw] aside and told him that they had no idea what they were in for, and we got out there and played good."

Marshall—an All-Pro defensive end—was completely shut down. He finished with no tackles, no assists, and never got close to Stabler as the Raiders beat the Vikings, 32–14, and finally won an NFL title.

For Shell and the Raiders, it was a day of redemption, a day to quiet the critics who had said that the Raiders, for all their toughness and bravado, couldn't win the big games.

Shell was tired of going to all those Pro Bowls where he had to hear the taunts from other players who wouldn't let him forget that the Raiders couldn't win a Super Bowl.

"The guys at the Pro Bowls would tell me that if you wanted to win a Super Bowl, then play the Raiders," Shell said. "But after we beat the Vikings, we finally arrived."

The week before the game, Shell knew the Raiders would win. He felt the crispness of the practices, the unspoken confidence among the players.

The Raiders' approach during Super Bowl week was not unlike that of any other regular-season game week. There was no curfew on Monday night, and Tuesday was picture day. On Wednesday, the veterans stood up and said the partying was over. The circle was closing around the team.

"We got all the craziness out of the way on Monday night and then we said that we didn't want to find anyone out on the streets, especially the young guys," Shell said.

"It was eerie. On Thursday, I don't think a pass hit the ground in practice all day, we were that sharp. And in the Wednesday defensive practice, I told Gene that if we played today, the Vikings wouldn't score a point. Then, on Friday and Saturday, we were loose. On Saturday, we had an hour review practice and we took a tape ball and played softball on the field. Al walked up and asked us what in the hell we were doing, but that's how loose and relaxed we were."

That year at the Pro Bowl, the taunting stopped.

"The Super Bowl was a game you strive to be in, and I felt that we had arrived and now we could do more damage," Shell said. "Of course, the following year we had the fumble in Denver, but I felt we could have gone on and won the Super Bowl. But then things started to fall apart."

In 1979, Shell suffered his first major injury, tearing the medial collateral ligament in his knee and ending his remarkable string of 207 games played.

The Raiders rebounded in the 1980 season with another Super Bowl win, but the wear and tear was beginning to show.

"Around 1979 I could feel I wasn't the same. Still, my leg was good through 1980 and I was effective. When you play the game, you know your skills are going to diminish, although you can continue playing."

In 1982, he could feel the end coming. Upshaw was injured and things were no longer the same. Shell had lost some quickness and he still tried to muster the same drive, but during a morning practice in training camp in 1982, he ran a play and the blocks that once seemed so easy came harder.

"I went out and hit this guy and it didn't happen the way I wanted, so I asked to run the play again and I still didn't get what I wanted," Shell said. "I could have played, but I didn't want to hang on. But I knew it was time when Marcus Allen came to me in 1982 and said that he was seven years old when I first played in the league."

Shell retired that year, but he wasn't about to leave football.

From the beginning of his career, Shell had made no secret of his desire to coach. As a player, he had impressed John Madden with his study habits and his knowledge of the game. Toward the end of his career, he told the Raiders' owner of his plan to coach.

Davis had told Shell that when it was time, he would help. And Davis kept his word. In 1983, Shell was named the Raiders' offensive line coach, and in 1989, he got the chance he had dreamed about since he retired as a player.

A few months after Shell was inducted into the Pro Football Hall of Fame, Davis fired Mike Shanahan and named Shell as the Raiders' head coach the next day. Shell became the NFL's first black head coach since Fritz Pollard coached the Hammond, Indiana, Pros from 1923 to 1925.

"Al called me late one night, and it was unexpected. I was suprised by the timing of it. But I knew it was a situation to win and where I didn't have to worry about being black. Al hired me not because I was black, but because I was a Raider."

Though the Raiders had moved south to Los Angeles, Shell tried to instill some of the old Raiders tradition into the organization and it worked. He won seven games in 1989 after taking over the team, and over the next four years, the Raiders made the playoffs three times.

But it wasn't an easy transition for Shell. As an assistant coach, you deal with just your position players. As a head coach, you deal with everything.

"The toughest part is that you're not a hands-on coach anymore. You're in charge of everything from travel to the time the players go to bed. As an assistant coach, you mingle a lot more with the players and staff, but as the head coach, people stay away. It becomes lonely."

Under Shell's leadership, the Raiders regained some of their swagger and in 1990, he was named NFL Coach of the Year after leading the team to a 12–4 record and to the AFC championship game, where they lost to the Buffalo Bills 51–3.

Shell's coaching style was the same as his style when he played.

"Screaming and hollering wasn't me," he said. "I wouldn't embarrass them, and I expected them not to embarrass me. And if you weren't on time, then you had big problems with me."

Though Shell led the Raiders to three playoff appearances during his tenure, it wasn't enough. In 1994, when the Raiders slipped to a 9–7 record, Davis fired him, hiring Mike White with the hope of reviving the Raiders' offense.

After 27 years, Shell was through with the Raiders.

"When Al fired me, it was tough on him to tell me and it took a while. By the time I was let go, there weren't many jobs open," Shell said. "But then Kansas City offered me the defensive line coach job, and I took it."

Suddenly, Shell was the enemy.

"That was really strange to go to Kansas City and put that red outfit on, and it was different for my wife Janice and my two kids after living in one place for 27 years, but Kansas City really opened their arms up to us. It was unbelievable."

After two seasons in Kansas City, Shell returned to his native South by joining the Falcons' staff. He plans to someday land another head coaching job in the still lily-white NFL head coaching ranks.

"The problem for us [black coaches] is getting the opportunity to sit down and talk with owners so they can find a different side to us," Shell said. "If you don't get the opportunity to sit down with an owner, then how will you get the chance to become a head coach?"

Shell knows the odds are historically against him.

He's getting older while caucasian head coaches are getting hired younger.

"I'd like to think that I'll get another chance someday," he said. "My life is pretty simple. I am working in an area that I love, and I don't really have a lot of big hobbies. All my life I wanted to coach, and nothing thrills me more than seeing young guys do well. But you know what? I'll always be a Raider."

Arthur (Art) Shell

Born November 26, 1946, at Charleston, SC
Height: 6′5″ Weight: 285
High School: North Charleston, SC, Bonds–Wilson.
Received bachelor of science degree in industrial arts education from
Maryland State–Eastern Shore College in 1968.

Named to *The Sporting News* AFC All-Star Team, 1974, 1975, and 1976.

Selected by Oakland AFL in 3rd round (80th player selected) of 1968 AFL-NFL draft.

On injured reserve with knee injury, August 29 through October 7, 1979; activated, October 8, 1979.

Oakland AFL, 1968 and 1969; Oakland NFL, 1970 through 1981; Los Angeles Raiders NFL, 1982.

Games: 1968 (14), 1969 (14), 1970 (14), 1972 (14), 1973 (14), 1974 (14), 1975 (14), 1976 (14), 1977 (14), 1978 (16), 1979 (11), 1980 (16), 1981 (16), 1982 (8). Total AFL—28, Total NFL—179, Total Pro—207.

Pro statistics: Fumbled once and returned one punt for no yards, 1968; recovered one fumble, 1970, 1971, and 1977; recovered two fumbles, 1978; recovered one fumble for five yards, 1979; recovered three fumbles, 1980.

Played in Pro Bowl following 1972 through 1978 and 1980 seasons.

Played in AFL Championship Game, 1969.

Played in AFC Championship Game following 1970, 1973 through 1977, and 1980 seasons.

Played in NFL Championship Game following 1976 and 1980 seasons.

JOHN MADDEN in a calm moment on the sidelines

4

JOHN MADDEN

There may be no place better suited for John Madden than a hotel lobby, except maybe the well-outfitted interior of the well-known Madden Cruiser bus that ferries him around the country because he refuses to travel by air.

Madden's celebrity status as the nation's top football announcer has attracted corporate sponsors eager to attach their names to the bus that takes him around the country to his weekly assignments during the NFL season for the Fox network. Synergy, sports marketers call their sponsorship of the bus. Madden calls it sheer convenience.

During the season, Madden spends his days on his bus or in hotel lobbies, where the wide assortment of people passing through appeals to his innate curiosity and gregarious nature.

Then again, who wouldn't want to loiter in places like the rustic elegance of the Biltmore Hotel lobby, where I introduced myself to him on an unseasonably cool Tuesday afternoon in Phoenix during the NFL's annual March spring meetings.

Make no mistake, the NFL travels first class and the Biltmore's lobby is a perfect place for Madden, except maybe for its classic Frank Lloyd Wright design that clashes with Madden's white sweat suit, Fox network baseball cap, and untied shoes with no socks.

Nonetheless, Madden sits in the lobby's cushy leather chairs, unlit cigar in hand, and holds court, talking to just about anyone who passes in his large shadow. And with the NFL in town, what better place for Madden to catch up with long-lost friends and distant acquaintances, which is exactly what he was doing when I introduced myself.

Madden, who was in Phoenix flying the Fox network's colors, was talking shop with television sports personality Lesley Visser, who was seeking his counsel about some project she was considering.

Along with his $30 million deal with Fox, Madden earns millions of dollars more as America's salesman, cashing in on Madison Avenue's allure to his "everyman" image that makes him a perfect guy to sell everything from hammers to foot spray.

Madden may come across as the guy sitting next to you in the corner tavern, but he's also a shrewd businessman who knows the value of his image. He has taken his celebrity and created a full-blown corporation out of himself. His video game is a top seller, his books sell well, and now he's multimedia, with his own radio show, and, naturally, his own website.

But even with all the celebrity, Madden's still a football coach, which is why he rescued the old, rusted Raiders blocking sled from the dumpster when the wrecking ball hit the team's former training camp site in Santa Rosa. Madden, who watched his players hit that sled every summer for a decade, stuck the sled in the backyard of his Pleasanton, California, home, where it sits to remind him of who he really is.

Upon my introduction, Madden immediately introduced me to Visser, who was friendly enough not to be bothered by the interruption. After I explained what I wanted, he took my card and wrote down a phone number to call him to arrange a meeting. Then he left for lunch.

Dozens of messages later, Madden returned my call out of the blue late one Friday afternoon. The friendly ladies who staff his office politely explained how busy he is and then promptly patched me through to him while he was driving around the Bay Area in his truck.

Whether analyzing a game for a national television audience or holding court in a hotel lobby, or talking to me across the country on a cell phone, his voice, manner, and style are the same. But when he begins to talk about the Raiders, he speaks a little faster and becomes more football coach than Emmy Award–winning television commentator.

Given his two decades on the air, twice as long as he coached the Raiders, there is a generation of football fans who know John Madden simply as a sometimes overzealous football announcer with an inimitable style that displays his passion for the game. But lost amid the cult of his television personality is a remarkable professional coaching career that began with the Raiders in 1967 when he was all of 31 years old.

Madden grew up the son of a mechanic in Daly City, California, a working-class town just south of San Francisco. After graduating in 1958 from Cal Poly–San Luis Obispo, where he was an all-conference offensive and defensive lineman, he was drafted by the Philadelphia Eagles in the 21st round. His days as a pro were numbered after he ripped the ligaments in his right knee during training camp. The next year, he turned to coaching. It took him all of six years to land a professional football coaching job.

In 1967, after spending two years as a defensive coordinator at San Diego State University, he was hired on as the Raiders' linebackers coach, a far cry from his days as a head coach at Hancock Junior College in Santa Maria, California, where in the 1962 and 1963 seasons he compiled a 13–5 record.

His quick rise to the professional level may have been an anomaly, but he was smart, he was likable, and he was utterly without pretense. No matter the level, players immediately picked up on his nature, which allowed Madden to gain their trust and, more important, their confidence.

In 1969, he convinced Al Davis that he was the man to replace John Rauch as the Raiders' head coach. Though Rauch had brought the Raiders to Super Bowl I in January 1968, he and Davis were at odds and Rauch left the Raiders after the 1968 season for a job with the Buffalo Bills.

Madden, convinced that at age 33 he was qualified, went to Davis and won the head coaching job. It was a bold move, given he had all of two years' experience coaching professional football.

"I was so young that I thought I knew everything," Madden said. "Hell, I thought I should win every game, and I had a lot of confidence. It helped that in my first year as head coach we only lost one game, so I got off to a good start. But I don't know if I would have hired me."

The Raiders went 12–1–1 in Madden's first year, losing to the Kansas City Chiefs, 17–7, in the AFL's last championship game. It was the beginning of a wildly successful, yet frustrating, 10-year run for Madden and the Raiders. Under his tenure as the Raiders' head coach, they went to the playoffs in eight of the ten seasons, winning more than 100 games and one Super Bowl. Still, when a burned-out Madden retired in 1979, he had a regular-season record of 103 wins, 32 losses, and 7 ties. His playoff record was a mediocre 9–7, but he was the first NFL coach to reach 100 wins in 10 years.

Much of the credit for the Raiders' success went to Davis, but Madden didn't need the attention or particularly care about recognition. His ego could take a backseat to Davis's and he was comfortable with his style of coaching that treated his players as individuals, saving judgment for the football field.

When I asked him how he handled the players, Madden sounded insulted.

"First of all, I never used the word *handle*," he said. "And I never handled anybody. The players were all individuals, and I respected them as individuals and got them to play together as a team. Remember that during the 1970s coaches had a lot of rules: you couldn't have facial hair, you had to wear a shirt and tie on the road, you couldn't sit on your helmet, and stuff like that. But I had just three rules: be on time, pay attention, and play like hell on Sundays."

It was more complicated than that. Madden knew his players, knew how to treat each one. Where he'd never yell at Art Shell, he'd jump all over Gene Upshaw, knowing that he'd respond. He let Ted Hendricks get away with riding a horse on a practice field and tolerated other antics as long as he got what he wanted from each player. And if John Matuszak wanted to booze all day on his Terrible Toozday off days during the season, that was okay as long as Matuszak produced on Sunday.

"Guys like Ted were the easiest guys to coach, because they played hard on Sunday and rarely made mistakes," Madden said.

"I always took the week backwards. You take the week from Sunday and work back from there. So what if Ted wanted to wear an Army helmet on Wednesday. That kind of stuff never bothered me, because he played like hell on Sunday. But it wasn't like we didn't have any discipline. We had football discipline. We never jumped offsides. We worked long and hard in training camp, and we didn't do stupid stuff on the field. Hell, we were in camp for two months, and when I tell players that today, they laugh at how hard we worked."

Madden made himself available to his players. He'd spend time with them in camp, get to know them, their wives, their kids, and their problems. He wasn't some sort of feel-good camp counselor, he'd just make sure he was around.

"I got to know them in a different way," Madden said. "I always thought the lines of communication were open, and we'd do stuff together. We'd have parties at the Hilton, and later we'd all go down to Jack London Square together. I knew the single guys, I knew the married guys, and I made a habit of being available to every player every day. That way nothing would fester."

Madden's style worked. From 1973 through 1977, the Raiders played in five consecutive AFC championship games, and with the wins came the Raiders' mystique, enhanced by the organization's covert method of operations. Madden was crafty enough to rally the Raiders around their reputation.

"That goes back to the AFL days and when there was the recruiting of players and hiding them and all that stuff," Madden said. "We were the inferior league, and after that we kept the attitude going. I felt it was an advantage and helped us get ready for a game. I would always narrow down the circle as the games got closer. We'd have people around early in the week, and then as the week progressed, we'd only have players and coaches around. Whether that was paranoia or the us-against-them philosophy, we believed in it and we played that way."

Solidified by a nucleus of talent ranging from old-timers like George Blanda and Jim Otto to steady performers like Fred Biletnikoff and Pete Banaszak, Madden was able to successfully restock the team through the draft, though the Raiders took a different approach compared to that of other teams.

Ignoring scouting combines and, later, shared information among teams, the Raiders' picks would leave outsiders scratching their heads.

More often than not, the Raiders ignored players from the football factories and instead took chances on guys like Shell, Upshaw, Mark van Eeghen, and other unheralded players that nobody had heard of.

Not that Davis and the Raiders were always successful. For every Art Shell, who as the Raiders' 1968 third-round pick would find his way into the Hall of Fame, there were busts like Ted Koy, the team's second-round pick in 1970 who couldn't stick with the team.

Unlike other teams, the Raiders weren't all that sophisticated when it came to the draft. There were certain qualities that had to be found, but there was also the sense of the intangible—that is, whether Madden, Davis, and general manager Ron Wolf deemed a player "Raider material."

It wasn't just a strategy employed during the draft. Madden never flinched when taking chances on players like Matuszak or Hendricks, both of whom the Raiders rescued from the NFL scrap heap.

"We signed Matuszak and we had a bunch of free spirits, but we didn't build our team around guys like that," Madden said. "And we had our hits and misses. Basically, Al or Ron Wolf had to have a good feel for the player. But the players had to be either big or fast. That was the thing. That's why we took Art Shell and Cliff Branch. They also had to be tough or I wasn't going to play them. But we had such a good core of players that we had to figure if a new guy would fit in or if they had to lead the band.

"But I had so many good players, sometimes you just wondered how it all happened. There was George Atkinson, who wore glasses and played at 160 pounds, and you'd think how in the hell can he hit so hard. And some of the passes that Stabler threw, and how Dave Casper did so much. We had so many Hall of Fame players."

Not that there weren't any internal battles between Davis, Wolf, and Madden over draft picks and personnel moves. Madden would want one guy, and Wolf another, and Davis still another. But Madden knew how to get along with Davis. He understood him and his propensity for controlling the organization.

"We had a very natural relationship, and Al is one of the best friends I have in the world," Madden said. "Al had a reputation, and it was fun for a coach because anything we did, people always blamed Al. Shit, it was great for me, because he got blamed for everything and I had the freedom to do what I wanted."

Madden was working in the NFL during an era that suited his personality. Team operations were smaller and simpler. There was no salary cap, no free agency, and much less media scrutiny to contend with.

A head coach could simply operate as a head coach and was unburdened by the administrative duties that today's head coaches must deal with.

"You have to remember that 30 years ago, we had five-man coaching staffs and a one-man scouting department. Our entire organization was the coaches, Ron Wolf, and Al. We were together all the time, and we didn't have a boardroom or anything like that. We'd bring in the food, lay it out, and that was that. Now head coaches are CEOs."

Still, it wasn't as if he approached his job with the Raiders like he was back at Hancock Junior College.

Madden would allow his players latitude, but come Sunday, he'd be a wreck on the sidelines, charging up and down the bench, waving his arms, red-faced and full of anxiety. It was entertaining for the cameras, and it won him a Miller Lite beer commercial, but the games tore at his insides.

"The wins didn't mean all that much, but when we'd lose it would be a shock," Madden said. "But the toughest loss was probably the Immaculate Reception game against Pittsburgh in the 1972 AFC playoff game. It was just so final. There was no next week."

It took ultracool Ken Stabler to counterbalance Madden's manic style on the sidelines, but the combination worked. Stabler had complete respect for Madden, and Madden had full confidence in Stabler.

"As a coach, I was very emotional and volatile," Madden said. "As a player, Kenny was very calm. If we were both like me, we would have never gotten anything done. His calmness really off-set me."

It was Stabler who would go to Madden during the drudgery of training camp and tell Madden and the coaches to ease up. And Madden would instinctively know when to ease his throttle on the team while keeping command of the players. If he sensed a problem with a particular player, he'd pull aside a veteran like Jim Otto and the problem would be taken care of.

"I swear I never knew how it was done," Madden said. "But that was the type of leadership we had on the team."

Though the Raiders went to the Super Bowl just once during Madden's career, he offers no apologies. To him, the Raiders never choked and were never unprepared, they just lost to better teams.

"We were real good, but so was Pittsburgh and so was Miami, and now so many of their players are in the Hall of Fame. I mean, it wasn't like we were losing to bad teams."

The ultimate for Madden, of course, was the Super Bowl win over the Minnesota Vikings, but for him, that wasn't the best game the Raiders played.

"It was [week two] in 1977, the year after we won the Super Bowl and we had beaten the Steelers in the playoffs and we went in and beat them again," Madden said of the Raiders' 16–7 victory. "It was like a war or a 25-round heavyweight fight. Stabler got hurt and so did [linebacker] Phil Villapiano, and we lost other players for a while, but we never played better. We got to the AFC championship game later that year against Denver, but we were too beat up. But that early-season Pittsburgh game was the peak."

The loss to Denver in the 1977 AFC championship game was the first crack in what would soon be the end of the Raiders' dominance in the AFC West.

Though the Raiders went into Denver in 1977 leading the league in virtually every offensive and defensive category, they couldn't finish off the Broncos to make consecutive Super Bowl appearances.

And again, the 1977 AFC championship game put the Raiders at the center of controversy.

With a 7–3 lead in the third quarter, Denver running back Rob Lytle took a handoff from Craig Morton at the Raiders' two-yard line and was drilled at the line of scrimmage by safety Jack Tatum, who jarred the ball loose.

Raiders defensive lineman Mike McCoy scooped up the ball and was running toward Denver's end zone, only to have the officials blow the play dead, ruling that Lytle had not fumbled. But television replays showed the ball popping out of Lytle's arms, costing the Raiders a forced turnover. The Broncos scored on the next play, and the Raiders never recovered, losing, 20–17.

It was the last playoff appearance for the Raiders under Madden. The Raiders finished second in the AFC West in 1978 with a 9–7 record, and at the end of the season, Madden had had enough. The stress and the pressure of his 10 seasons as head coach had taken its toll, with Madden suffering from ulcers and unable to work up the energy to handle another season. In late December, he went to Davis and told him he was considering leaving the Raiders.

"It wasn't something that was prethought," Madden said. "I just had put in 10 years and won over 100 games, and I couldn't see myself going through it again. You have to start all over and be excited about the draft and minicamps. Back then, there were no words like *burnout*. I just had the feeling, and I told Al that I didn't want to do it anymore. But there was no friction between me and Al."

Davis, who thought Madden was overtired from the rigors of what had been a disappointing Raiders season, told Madden to keep his mouth shut and take a week to think about it. After a week in Las Vegas, Madden hadn't changed his mind.

In January 1979, Madden announced his retirement and Davis named Tom Flores as the new head coach. Madden, who had no firm plans at the time, was hired by CBS as a football analyst. Suddenly, Madden was prospering in a job he couldn't have imagined holding a year earlier.

But it's still just television to Madden.

It's the football that still excites him. It's a player bouncing up from a tackle with a hunk of turf stuck to his face mask, a lineman coming off the field full of dirt and mud, that brings him back to Oakland.

"Those teams were not selfish," Madden said. "Nobody worried about the number of carries per game and yards and all that stuff. And when Fred Biletnikoff's daughter was killed in the spring of 1999, all the players came to the funeral. Pete Banaszak flew in from Florida, Jack Tatum came, and Willie Brown was an usher. I was thinking during the service that after so many years, they still rally for each other."

John Earl Madden

Born April 10, 1936, at Austin, MN
High School: Daly City, CA, Jefferson.
Attended College of San Mateo and received bachelor of science degree in 1959
and master of arts degree in 1961 from California Polytechnic College at San Luis Obispo.

Selected (as future choice) by Philadelphia in 21st round of 1958 NFL draft.
Suffered knee injury during first training camp, 1959.

COACHING RECORD

Named by *The Sporting News* as AFL Coach of the Year for 1969.
Assistant coach, Allan Hancock College, 1960 and 1961.
Assistant coach, San Diego State College, 1964 through 1966.
Assistant coach, Oakland Raiders, 1967 and 1968.

Year	Club	Pos.	W.	L.	T.
1962	Hancock College	†Second	4	5	0
1963	Hancock College	†First	8	1	0
1969	Oakland AFL	‡First	12	1	1
1970	Oakland NFL	§First	8	4	2
(Won conference playoff game from Miami, 21–14; lost conference to Baltimore, 27–17.)					
1971	Oakland NFL	§Second	8	4	2
1972	Oakland NFL	§First	10	3	1
(Lost conference playoff game to Pittsburgh, 13–7.)					
1973	Oakland NFL	§First	9	4	1
(Won conference playoff game from Pittsburgh, 33–14; lost conference championship game to Miami, 27–10.)					
1974	Oakland NFL	§First	12	2	0
(Won conference playoff game from Miami, 28–26; lost conference championship game to Pittsburgh, 24–13.)					
1975	Oakland NFL	§First	11	3	0
(Won conference playoff game from Cincinnati, 31–28; lost conference championship game to Pittsburgh, 16–10.)					
1976	Oakland NFL	§First	13	1	0
(Won conference playoff game from New England, 24–21; won conference championship game from Pittsburgh, 24–7.)					
1977	Oakland NFL	§Second	11	3	0
(Won conference playoff game from Baltimore in overtime, 37–31; lost conference championship game to Denver, 20–17.)					
1978	Oakland NFL	§xSecond	9	7	0
AFL Totals—1 Year			12	1	1
NFL Totals—9 Years			91	31	6
Pro Totals—10 Years			103	32	7

Championship Game Coaching Record

1969   AFL—Oakland lost to Kansas City, 17–7.
1976   NFL—Oakland defeated Minnesota, 32–14.

†Central California Community College Athletic Association (Central Conference)
‡Western Division.
§Western Division (American Conference).
xTied for position.

Poetry in motion as **RAY GUY** blasts another punt skyward

5

RAY GUY

Ray Guy was born in the South, went to college in the South, and returned to the South in each offseason during his entire 14-year career as the Raiders' punter.

When Guy retired from the Raiders in 1987, he promptly moved his family back to Hattiesburg, Mississippi, where he attended Southern Mississippi University. Then he moved his family back to his native Thomson, Georgia, population 15,000, located just off Interstate 20 about two hours east of Atlanta.

He is, self-admittedly, a small-town man. He tolerated Oakland, which compared to other NFL cities is a small town, and he hated Los Angeles, where he was forced to live when the Raiders left Oakland in the early 1980s.

"Didn't like L.A.," Guy said. "I was never into the Hollywood nightlife where everybody is trying to be somebody else. I like a country atmosphere and the slow pace."

Which leads us to his theory as to why the Raiders won all those games back in the 1970s and had more fun than anyone while doing it.

It's a simple theory, really, one that won't satisfy those who think that building the team was some product of genius.

"Really, when you look at those teams, the reason we won and got along was that we were all from small towns," Guy said. "We all kinda came from the same place."

Right down the line, he is pretty much on the mark.

Guy, of course, hailed from Thomson.

The rest of the Raiders' core group, which consisted of Ken Stabler, Willie Brown, Fred Biletnikoff, Art Shell, Gene Upshaw, Pete

Banaszak, Jim Otto, and George Atkinson, all hailed from small towns.

Guy explains his theory over coffee and cigarettes on a Saturday morning in a Thomson hotel bar where, hours earlier, couples in cowboy boots line-danced to tired Garth Brooks songs.

"Better put another pot on, darling," Guy said to the woman at the hotel desk when he first walked into the bar.

Guy was one of the best athletes on the Raiders, and he still looks it.

He's got long arms and legs and a weathered, narrow face framed with large eyes. Though it's a warm, late-summer day, he is wearing a pair of jeans, a neatly pressed Raiders golf shirt, and a pair of white athletic shoes, and he is carrying his ever-present white Styrofoam cup filled with coffee. That and a pack of cigarettes are Guy's constant companions.

A standout defensive back in college, Guy couldn't stand to be considered just a kicker with the Raiders.

He'd work with the defensive backs in practice and was the Raiders' emergency quarterback. On kickoffs and punts, he held on to a perverse hope that he'd have to make a tackle so he could drill the ballcarrier.

Unlike many punters, Guy wouldn't wear flimsy shoulder pads, or a face mask with just one bar across the front. Instead, he would wear a full set of pads, including knee and thigh pads, during games, and his helmet had a full face mask. He considered himself a football player, not simply a punter, and demanded to be treated as such.

But Guy's body type was tailor-made to punt a football. At a lean 6 feet 3, 195 pounds, with long arms and legs, he could generate tremendous power in his hips, enabling him to blast the ball great distances, or create seemingly endless hang time. It also allowed Guy to throw 90-mile-per-hour fastballs as a high school baseball star.

Born with such natural gifts, the only kicking instruction he ever had was his high school coach telling him how to drop the ball to his foot.

"He just helped me drop the ball so I could kick a spiral," Guy said. "That's all the instruction I really needed."

As we talked, Guy drank endless amounts of coffee while lighting up one Marlboro after another.

He told me of the old-line families in town, which families owned the land, and how he had zero interest in the upcoming annual fox and hounds hunt where Thomson's gentry would put on red and black coats and chase a fox—or, if none was to be had, a frantic coyote—into the woods until everyone was too drunk to care anymore.

After hearing him tell me about the town, I asked for a tour and he agreed, though he probably would have just as soon gone back home to finish painting the new porch he put on the front of his house a few weeks before.

But Guy is nothing but a gentleman, so he ferried me around Thomson on a sleepy Saturday morning in his black Ford 150 pickup truck, pointing out areas of interest in between drags of his cigarette.

It was not one of those return-to-glory drives.

In fact, Guy seems to take the town simply for what it is—a town in transition after thriving in the 1960s when most of the nation's goods were made in places just like it.

But things changed after manufacturers began to take the work out of those small towns and into other countries where labor comes cheaper. Then giants like Wal-Mart came in on cheap land outside of town and drove mom-and-pop retailers into oblivion.

Now the only area of town that thrives is a stretch of road just off the interstate where filling stations, fast-food restaurants, and budget hotels rely on travelers for business.

Guy's not saying much as we circle around town. He's a bit annoyed by road construction along the highway and he's always on the lookout for speeders.

"Watch it, fool," he says if he sees someone driving too fast. In fact, when we talked on the phone making plans to meet, Guy had warned me to watch out for Atlanta drivers.

"It's like the Indy 500 down here," he had said.

So we drive. Guy, cigarette tucked in the corner of his mouth and his half-full coffee cup secured in a plastic cup holder, isn't pumping any one place or another.

He's simply showing what's what.

"Not much to it," Guy said, taking a sip from the coffee cup.

There's the new high school, there's a shuttered textile mill where the locals used to buy clothes cheap at the outlet store, and there's the old building materials plant where Guy's dad bought his home-building supplies and where Guy worked in high school. The place is in ruins now, the roof sagging and the paint peeling, and Guy doesn't say a word as we drive by.

But when we drive by the high school football field, an ancient place dubbed "The Brickyard," Guy turns into a docent.

"This place is so full of tradition that the locals refused to support a new field when the new high school was built a few years ago," he said. "The Negro baseball leagues used to barnstorm here, and some of the townspeople helped build this place back during the Depression."

When we cruise through the main drag, there is a strip of mostly boarded-up or empty storefronts located directly across a set of railroad tracks.

"Trains don't stop here anymore," Guy said matter-of-factly. "But those stores used to be nice."

We pass a mural painted on what used to be a storefront.

The folks at the local chamber of commerce thought a mural might brighten up the place, might be a nice way to show off the pride of Thomson and what it had to offer. So they had the wall painted in bright colors depicting all that's good in town: horses jumping, people shopping, and farmers. Also there, in full Raider uniform, is Guy. It's somewhat of a crude depiction, but the artist got it mostly right by painting Guy with his right leg jackknifed from the rest of his body, nearly parallel to his face as the ball sails off his foot.

Back in the late 1960s, Guy was one of the state's storied school-boy athletes as he starred for the Thomson Bulldogs. The locals still remember, because back then the town shut down at noon on Fridays during the football season to prepare for the games. Though Thomson's not Texas, high school football dominates the local landscape, and Ray Guy was a legend. So were his two older brothers, Al and Larry, who also played.

Son of the south: Ray Guy back in his native Thomson, Georgia.

"They kicked it farther than I did," Guy said.

He was an all-state quarterback, played safety, and was a baseball pitcher who got drafted by the Cincinnati Reds after his senior year. He won 16 high school letters. And, oh yeah, he punted and kicked field goals on the football team.

In the three years Guy played on the varsity, the Bulldogs won two state championships and lost just one game after a defender jumped on a teammate's back and managed to deflect Guy's field-goal attempt, ending the Bulldogs' streak.

"Years later, I was in the Atlanta airport one day when a guy came up to me and told me he was the guy who blocked the kick," Guy said. "I told him I'm still mad at 'im."

Though Guy was the local hero, he didn't act the part. How could he when his father, B.F., short for Benjamin Franklin, would have him on the job at six o'clock in the morning the day after a game, helping build houses?

Work was as much a part of Ray Guy's childhood as sports. Before B.F. moved the family into town, the Guys lived on a 350-

acre farm in neighboring Warren County. Then, when they moved to Thomson, Ray spent summers and weekends framing houses with his father.

"My dad always told me that if I started a job, then I'd better finish it, and he meant it. There was none of that sitting around on a Saturday and analyzing the high school football game. I was up at six on Saturday mornings. There were houses to build."

But it was obvious that Guy wouldn't be building houses for too long.

His high school stardom won him offers from practically every major college in the South. He passed on all but Southern Mississippi, where he could also play on the baseball team.

"I didn't like the big-college life, and as soon I stepped on campus, I felt comfortable," he said. "It felt like I was still in Thomson."

At Southern Miss, Guy played safety and kicked on the football team and was a star pitcher on the baseball team.

In three varsity seasons, Guy had 18 interceptions, kicked a 61-yard field goal, and was drafted four times by big league baseball teams.

"I played for the full enjoyment of playing," Guy said. "It never entered my mind to be a kicker. It was just something I did to help the team. I was a free safety, and I loved it."

Despite Guy's skills as a defensive back, it was his right leg that drew the NFL's interest.

In college, Guy had a 93-yard punt against the University of Mississippi, and he led the nation in punting as a senior in 1972 with a 46.2 average and was named to the All-America team.

But Guy's NFL future was put in jeopardy when, in his last game as a senior against Nicholls State University, a defender's blind-sided hit broke his left leg in two places above the ankle.

The injury cost Guy trips to the East-West Shrine Game and the Senior Bowl, where he would have been exposed to a bevy of NFL scouts, upping his value in the draft.

"You talk about seeing your future go right by," Guy said. "Luckily, I didn't get hit when I was kicking. The guy down the field had called a fair catch, and I was looking at the sideline getting the defensive call. Next thing I know, I was looking at the sun."

While the nation's other collegiate All-Americans showed their stuff in the postseason games, Guy, wounded leg and all, got married to Beverly, his hometown sweetheart, who was all of 18 when she married him.

When draft day rolled around, Guy was unsure of his status, but he had an ace in the hole. If the NFL ignored him, he had major league baseball to pursue.

Just to be safe, Southern Miss officials installed a phone in Guy's apartment the week before the draft. Newly married but still in school, Guy couldn't afford a phone.

The first hint that the Raiders were interested came the morning before the draft. A Raiders scout traveled to Hattiesburg and knocked on the newlyweds' door at six-thirty in the morning to check Guy out.

"I had just gotten my cast off and I had no idea the guy was coming," Guy said. "John Madden had sent him to check me out, but he never even asked how my leg was. An hour later he was back in New Orleans, calling John to tell him I looked fine."

The next day, Guy got an even bigger surprise when he received a call from Madden on a tinny speakerphone telling him the Raiders would choose him in the first round, the 23rd pick overall.

"Coach Madden called and said 'We've drafted you number one,' and I almost fell out of my chair," Guy said. "Then I had to figure out where Oakland, California, was. I thought it was someplace up in Wisconsin. This was early in the AFL, I didn't know the Oakland Raiders."

The Raiders first flew Guy to Los Angeles where he was examined by the team's orthopedic surgeon, Dr. Robert Rosenfeld, a good friend of owner Al Davis.

Guy got a clean bill of health and then flew to Oakland to start training camp after playing in the College All-Star Game where he was named MVP.

When he arrived in Santa Rosa, he was met by his new teammates and dozens of reporters wanting to see why the Raiders spent a first-round pick on a punter—something no other team had done before.

"When I walked onto the practice field for the first time, it seemed like there were 500 reporters waiting for me, asking all kinds of questions," Guy said. "But it was strange. The Raiders treated me like I had been there for years. The first guy I met was George Blanda, and we hit it off because I wasn't a threat."

The Raiders had already cut Jerry DePoyster, who had kicked for the Raiders in 1972, so it wasn't as if Guy had to win a job, but he had to prove himself in front of the skeptical media and curious teammates. It took about 10 minutes.

"The returners lined up on the 35-yard line, but after every punt, they kept backing up," Guy said. "I knew the press was looking at me, but I had great hang time that day."

The problem for Guy was boredom. He was used to playing defense and couldn't stand all the standing around he did as a kicker.

He ran pass patterns with the scout offense, he practiced with the defensive backs and did everything he could do to stay involved.

"That was real tough for me," Guy said. "In college I played every down, but I was used to doing everything. The first day I stepped out on the field in a seven-by-seven drill without even thinking. Fred [Biletnikoff] was getting ready to run a pass pattern and John Madden saw what was happening and started screaming at me."

Guy, a good old boy, fit right in with the Raiders and the lifestyle.

"I liked to have a good time, and I still do," Guy said. "I just don't do it as often as I did. I drank my beer, but I know a lot of people who didn't play professional sports and they had a helluva better time than I did."

Any talk that the Raiders wasted a first-round draft choice on a punter was quieted in training camp, but Guy picked a *Monday Night Football* telecast to raise new questions.

In the early 1970s, Guy handled the kickoffs as well as the punting. In that Monday night game early in Guy's rookie season against the Denver Broncos, George Blanda kicked a 49-yard field goal with 36 seconds remaining to put the Raiders on top, 23–20.

Then Guy distinguished himself in front of a national audience.

On the ensuing kickoff, he booted the ball out of bounds. Penalized 10 yards, he kicked off again and once more he booted the ball out of bounds, forcing a third kickoff that gave the Broncos good field position. A few plays later, Broncos kicker Jim Turner hit a 35-yard field goal with three seconds left and the game ended in a 23–23 tie.

But that was one of Guy's rare errors. He made the All-Pro team as a rookie, the first of seven All-Pro appearances, six of which were in consecutive years, from 1973 to 1978.

The Raiders' record book is peppered with records set by Guy.

He led the NFL in punting average in 1974, '75, and 1977, and he holds the Raiders' record for most career punts with 1,049 for a record 44,493 yards. In his rookie year, he set the Raiders' single-season punt-distance average record with a 45.3-yard average, and he holds the single-game record with a 57.6 average, set against the Broncos in 1981. His career punting average is 42.4 yards per kick, and he played in three Super Bowls and seven AFC championship games.

His ability to generate hang time with his kicks is legendary. Guy was the first punter to hit the scoreboard suspended from the roof of the Louisiana Superdome.

"I can count the number of blocked kicks on one hand," he said, and he's right. He once went 619 punts without a block, and he had only three blocked punts in 1,049 career punts, a testament to his quick leg and the good protection he received.

Unfortunately, the first blocked punt came in the Raiders Super Bowl game against the Vikings.

It was fourth-down from the Raiders' 34-yard line. The Vikings blocked the punt and recovered the ball on the Raiders' three-yard line. The Vikings fumbled three plays later and the Raiders recovered, but the block still bothers Guy.

"They didn't even have the punt block on," he said. "I was so mad I could have bit a 20-penny nail."

Guy finally made up for the block in another Raiders Super Bowl appearance, against the Washington Redskins in 1984. He soared in the air to snare a high snap and got the punt off. The Raiders went on to beat the Redskins for Guy's third Super Bowl ring and, just as important, his third Super Bowl check.

After the 1984 Super Bowl, Guy could feel a change. Actually, it started when the Raiders moved south to Los Angeles in 1981, but by 1985, football was getting tiresome.

"The whole atmosphere had changed, something just didn't feel right, and I always said I would retire when it got to be like work," Guy said.

After the 1986 season, Guy was developing back problems that eventually put him in the hospital.

In May 1987, he told the Raiders he had had enough, walking away from the last year of a contract that would have paid him $300,000 in 1987. He was 38 years old, ancient by NFL standards.

"I knew it was coming, and after I announced in May, I never looked back," Guy said.

The first thing he did was to move out of Los Angeles and back to Hattiesburg, where he was a volunteer coach and helped out Southern Miss.

But after a few years, Guy grew restless, and when his father was stricken with cancer, Guy moved Beverly and their two children back to Thomson.

Back home, Guy soon took a job as a marketing representative for a wood products company, but the job involved too much travel. Today, he sells health insurance for AFLAC, with his book of business mainly in Florida.

He also conducts kicking classes around the South and hooks up with his former teammates for an occasional charity golf outing.

Every January during Super Bowl week, Guy pays a little more attention when his phone rings. That's the week when new members of the Pro Football Hall of Fame are elected, and Guy's been on the ballot since 1992.

But with no true punters and only one field goal kicker in the Hall of Fame, Guy's not banking on getting in.

"There are guys who should have been in years ago and aren't in," he said. "Guys like Kenny Stabler should be in, so I'm not going to die if I'm not in it. If it happens, it happens. Hopefully, I'll still be breathing when it happens."

William Ray Guy

Born December 22, 1949, at Swainsboro, GA
Height: 6'3" Weight: 205
High School: Thomson, GA.
Attended University of Southern Mississippi.

Named as punter on *The Sporting News* College All-America Team, 1972.
Named to *The Sporting News* AFC All Star Team, 1973 through 1978.
Selected by Oakland in 1st round (23rd player selected) of 1973 NFL draft.
Selected by Cincinnati Reds' organization in 14th round of free-agent draft, June 5, 1969.
Selected by Houston Astros' organization in secondary phase of free-agent draft, June 8, 1971.
Selected by Atlanta Braves' organization in 17th round of free-agent draft, June 6, 1972.
Selected by Cincinnati Reds' organization in secondary phase of free-agent draft, January 10, 1973.

		PUNTING			
Year	Club	G.	No.	Avg.	BLK.
1973	Oakland NFL	14	69	45.3	0
1974	Oakland NFL	14	74	*42.2	0
1975	Oakland NFL	14	68	*43.8	0
1976	Oakland NFL	14	67	41.6	0
1977	Oakland NFL	14	59	*43.3	0
1978	Oakland NFL	16	81	42.7	*2
1979	Oakland NFL	16	69	42.6	1
1980	Oakland NFL	16	71	43.6	0
1981	Oakland NFL	16	96	43.7	0
1982	Los Angeles Raiders NFL	9	47	39.1	0
1983	Los Angeles Raiders NFL	16	78	42.8	0
1984	Los Angeles Raiders NFL	16	91	41.9	0
1985	Los Angeles Raiders NFL	16	89	40.8	0
1986	Los Angeles Raiders NFL	16	90	40.2	0
	Pro Totals—14 years	207	1049	42.4	3

Additional pro statistics: Rushed once for 21 yards, 1973; fumbled once for minus seven yards and attempted one pass with one interception, 1974; attempted one pass with one completion for 22 yards, 1975; rushed once for no yards, 1976, 1985, and 1986; fumbled once for minus 14 yards and kicked one extra point after touchdown, 1976; recovered one fumble, 1976, 1980, and 1986; rushed three times for 38 yards and attempted one pass with one completion for 32 yards, 1980; fumbled once, 1981; rushed two times for minus three yards, 1982; rushed twice for minus 13 yards, 1983; fumbled once for minus 28 yards, 1985; fumbled once for minus 18 yards, 1986.

Played in AFC Championship Game following 1973 through 1977, 1980, and 1983 seasons.
Played in NFL Championship Game following 1976, 1980, and 1983 seasons.
Played in Pro Bowl following 1973 through 1978 and 1980 seasons.

THE MAD STORK
draws a bead on FRAN TARKENTON
in Super Bowl XI.

6

THE MAD STORK

Ted Hendricks

The morning is slate gray, but Ted Hendricks is all Miami in his Ray-Ban sunglasses, white shorts, and white golf shirt that sports the Green Bay Packers emblem on the sleeve. It's a shirt Hendricks got as a gift from playing in the Vince Lombardi charity golf tournament that's held each year near Green Bay, where former Packers gather, drink, and remember the glory days while raising a few dollars for a good cause.

Though Hendricks defined his career as a Raider, he was a member of the 1974 Packers, and that makes him an alum. He wouldn't miss the outing for anything.

Then again, he hasn't missed many of the dozens of charity golf outings sponsored each year by former players trying to make good on their past. For Hendricks, the golf outings are a staple: see old friends, connect with former players, have some beers, resurrect fading stories. For Hendricks and everybody else, the golf outings serve as a quick and effective transport back to the days of muddy helmets, hard-fought first downs, and goal-line stands, a world that Hendricks had mastered.

But today's golf outing isn't at all like the Lombardi tournament. No former players, no fans, no banquet, no gift bags. Just Hendricks, his girlfriend Linda, her brother, and me at a public course not yet recovered from a late-summer weekend of overbooked tee times.

Hendricks suggested we play golf after I called his number in Miami Springs, Florida, and left a message stating my purpose. He got back to me a few days later, and in his gruff voice said he was now living near Chicago and suggested that we meet at a course sandwiched in between look-alike tract subdivisions and apartment complexes in northwestern suburban Chicago.

Our golf date fell on the Monday after the Pro Football Hall of Fame induction ceremonies, and it must have been quite a comedown for Hendricks from the past weekend, which he'd spent in Canton, Ohio, surrounded by his faithful, ushering in a new class of Hall of Famers.

"Hell yes, I was there," he said of his Hall of Fame weekend. "I'm part owner of the place."

Damn right, he is. Hendricks was elected in the class of 1990, with Pittsburgh Steelers rivals Franco Harris and Jack Lambert, Miami Dolphins quarterback Bob Griese, and legendary Dallas Cowboys coach Tom Landry.

He was a shoo-in following a 15-year NFL career that began with the Baltimore Colts, followed by a year with the Packers, and finally nine years with the Raiders. Hendricks played in eight Pro Bowls, seven AFC title games, and four Super Bowls; most impressive of all, the gangly 6-foot-7-inch, 235-pound linebacker played in 215 consecutive games and never had major surgery. That's not to say that he never got hurt, it's just that he never let the injuries get in the way. His consecutive-game streak alone would have been enough to put him squarely in the Hall of Fame.

Hendricks still looks as if he could put on a helmet and start heaving blockers around like spent automobile tires. He's rangy, with arms and legs that are remarkably clear of scars, knots, and other assorted trauma one expects to see on someone who spent so much time sprinting across football fields, banging into other bodies at top speed. His nickname at Miami was The Mad Stork, but really, with such massive leverage from those long arms and legs, his body resembles a construction crane more than a delicate wading bird.

"Came out clean," Hendricks said, and physically he's right. He doesn't look all that much different now than he did under his helmet. He still has the full head of curly blondish hair, the mustache, and the piercing eyes that scared quarterbacks into throwing the ball a half-second sooner than they wanted to. About the only thing physically different about him now from his playing days is a paunch protruding from under his golf shirt.

As our foursome warily assembles at the starter shack, Hendricks breaks the ice a bit by mentioning that he's also a member of the Italian Hall of Fame. He explains that his mother's maiden name is Bonatti, giving him enough Italian blood to put him in the hall.

"Went in with Tommy Lasorda," he said with a laugh as he thoughtfully straps my bag next to his on the back of our cart. He's got a top-line set of clubs and bag made from the same leather as the official Wilson NFL game balls, no doubt another perk from one of the better-funded charity golf events.

After depositing a dip of chewing tobacco under his bottom lip, he motors us to the first tee and, without any delay, steps up and launches his drive into the thick overcast. He has a decent swing for such a big man, and a remarkably soft touch around the green, his mathematical mind almost unerring in this part of his game.

Hendricks was a mathematics and physics major at the University of Miami. He never graduated, he says, because he couldn't fully grasp the theoretical aspects of math. The quantitative stuff was a breeze for him; he graduated in the top 10 percent of his class at Hialeah High School, but it was the macrophysics concepts that gave him fits. An All-American at Miami, he left school without his degree.

His father Maurice, or "Sonny," was a mechanic for Pan Am Airlines and his mother Angela was a native of Guatemala City. Both worked for Pan Am when they met in Guatemala, eventually settling in Miami.

Hendricks, who was born in Guatemala in 1947, breezed through school, inheriting his father's mechanical mind. His free spirit was all his own.

But there is no Mad Stork in Hendricks today. No antics, no jokes. The man who ordered a Raiders trainer to carve up a pumpkin as a Raiders helmet so he could wear it out on the practice field on Halloween isn't at all apparent.

Neither is the man who would amble out to the practice field well before anyone else, stake a Cinzano wine umbrella into the turf, and while sitting under the shade, greet his teammates as they made their way onto the field.

Since his playing days ended in 1983, Hendricks hasn't been able to harness the same energy, the focus, the ability to find a worthwhile pursuit. He's been through a series of bad business deals and a divorce, as well as had a child out of wedlock.

He calls himself retired, but really, he's unoccupied.

"I'm enjoying life right now, and I'm happy, but I have to find something else to suit my personality," he said.

After our round of golf, Hendricks and I head to the grill, and over the course of five light beers, he hashes out his career. He's friendly and combative depending on the topic, but he's also honest about his career and his life after he retired.

"Football was a vehicle to express my personality and my freedom. I didn't have to answer to anybody," Hendricks said, hinting at why he hasn't been able to find himself since he retired. "For me, playing football was a luxury. I would have played for free."

But he didn't. When the Packers wouldn't give him a no-cut contact after he had what was probably his best year in football in 1974, he managed to get one out of Al Davis at $150,000 per year when he joined the Raiders in 1975.

Hendricks's rage against the NFL machine shouldn't have come as a surprise, given his penchant for quoting the poet William Blake, who, after all, was arrested on charges of sedition.

The Raiders didn't care about his interest in Blake or anything else, as long as he played every Sunday.

In a perfect bit of goofball symmetry, Hendricks wore number 83, former Raiders great Ben Davidson's old number.

"I was a five-year veteran and had been All-Pro for three years," Hendricks said. "I fit right into the Raiders system."

He was one of the league's misfits, a 6-foot-7 linebacker who came into the league at 215 skinny pounds. Despite the fact that Hendricks was a three-year All-American defensive end at the University of Miami, he wasn't exactly a hot NFL prospect.

The scouts couldn't peg him for any certain position. He was too light to be a defensive end and seemingly too tall and rangy to be a linebacker. But Hendricks was also agile, smart, and had

Ted Hendricks today, taking life as it comes

an uncanny instinct for the game. He just seemed to be able to make the plays when it counted the most.

Yet, for all his collegiate accomplishments and natural ability, Hendricks didn't get drafted until the second round of the 1969 draft, when the Baltimore Colts took the gamble.

"First of all, Joe Thomas, who was the general manager of the Miami Dolphins, was saying that he was going to make me the team's number one draft choice, but he drafted a guy named Bill Stanfill, who was a defensive end," Hendricks said. "If your hometown team passes you up, the rest of the teams get a little nervous and I thought I'd go in the second round. Low and behold, a Baltimore newspaper reporter called me up and told me I was drafted by the Colts. But I didn't know where they we going to play me. At the University of Miami, I was a stand-up defensive end, but I didn't have any pass coverage responsibilities; I was strictly a pass rusher. When I got to Baltimore, I was at the home of Georgia Rosenbloom (the wife of Carroll Rosenbloom, who owned the team), where we used a scale that was covered with some saffron or something to weigh me, and I weighed in at 214 pounds. When

I got to camp, Coach Shula had special drills to play outside, much to the chagrin of the veterans who had to stay after practice with me. When we broke camp, we used to eat lunch at Memorial Stadium and Shula would check on me, making me eat extra potatoes and ice cream."

Hendricks became an All-Pro with the Colts and the Raiders. Not only did he rack up the tackles, but in his career he had 26 interceptions, recovered 16 fumbles, and blocked 25 field goals and extra points. He also played in eight Pro Bowls and owns four Super Bowl rings.

His style was unorthodox. He roamed the field looking like a praying mantis, disrupting offenses with his long arms and uncanny instincts.

For Hendricks, having fun was just as much a part of being a Raider as playing hard.

Because he couldn't stand to lift weights, he would attach empty drums on each end of a barbell with "500 pounds" painted on the drums.

He once rode a horse onto the practice field, wielding a traffic cone as a lance. During a *Monday Night Football* game, he snuck a Halloween mask onto the field, slipping it over his face as the cameras panned the Raiders' bench.

His teammates went along with the hilarity, and as long as he produced, the coaches let him be.

"Madden was an offensive coach and left the defense alone," Hendricks said, adding that the one player who gave him the most difficulty was the Chicago Bears' Walter Payton.

"He was the hardest for me to tackle," he said. "I was so tall that most of my hits came from my shoulders, and he would keep bobbing and weaving."

Hendricks's best year with the Raiders may have been 1980, when he had a team-leading nine sacks, three interceptions, three blocked kicks, and a safety. He made his fifth All-Pro team that year.

"I had a lot of sacks and interceptions that year, but our goal was to just get into the playoffs," he said.

The Raiders not only made the playoffs as a wild-card team, but they went on to win the Super Bowl, trouncing the Philadelphia

Eagles, 27–10. It was Hendricks's second Super Bowl win with the Raiders and his third overall, as he played on the Baltimore Colts' Super Bowl V team in 1971. His play was so dominant in the 1981 Super Bowl that the Eagles' offense opted to run plays away from him to keep him from causing his usual mayhem.

"I had a pretty easy time in the Super Bowls," he said. "The first one, against Minnesota, I was the right defensive linebacker and that was the weak side of the Vikings' attack, so I came out with a clean uniform. I think I forced [the quarterback] to throw early, but that was about it. I also ran into the kicker on a punt block that gave the Vikings a first down and led to the first score of the game. Against the Eagles, [Coach Dick] Vermeil decided to not even bother going to the right side. But what I really remember from the Super Bowl is Vermeil saying that if players on his team were caught out past curfew, he'd send them home. But if that were us, we wouldn't have had any players left to play. We had a lot of fun in New Orleans, but we mixed it with business."

There seemed to be no end to Hendricks's antics, but eventually his skills declined along with his desire, and he retired at age 36 after the Raiders played in the 1984 Super Bowl.

"I'd just had enough of football and I was getting slower, but I left on my own terms," he said.

But Hendricks couldn't seem to make the adjustment from NFL star to former NFL star.

At one time, the possibilities seemed endless. He considered putting his math background to use.

"The space program sounded good," he said.

Instead, he has floundered. A golf course venture failed. Things just turned to Jell-O.

"A hurricane stalled business," he said.

Other ventures went bust, and so did his marriage to his former wife, Jane, with whom he has two sons. He also has a daughter with another woman.

Today, Hendricks is considering going back to school, but "I'm still in a holding pattern."

"Ted's doing a lot better," said his girlfriend's brother.

"Ted's where Ted wants to be," said former teammate Jim Otto, who has tried to step in and help.

For now, that means the charity and alumni golf tournament circuit, still hanging on to his Raiders days.

"I'm not certain what I'll do," Hendricks said. "It's hard for me to start over."

As a member of the NFL Hall of Fame, the owner of four Super Bowl rings, and part of an unbreakable link with Raiders, Hendricks can always cash in on autograph signings, celebrity cruises, and corporate golf outings that pay hefty appearance fees in exchange for shopworn stories of his Raiders days. Then there are the charities that Hendricks has been involved with, too big-hearted to turn down requests.

Fortunately, Hendricks, in the midst of all the partying and playing during his Raiders days, had the sense to buy some annuities that are now providing a financial cushion to go along with the paid appearances.

More than 15 years have passed since Hendricks retired, yet he is still looking for something to hold his interest. There has been no job, no career, after football. Decades of being defined as a football star have made it seemingly impossible for Hendricks to adapt to any semblance of a 9-to-5 routine, although some of his former teammates have arranged interviews, provided contacts, and given recommendations for him.

"I'm pursuing some other things and trying to find new interests," Hendricks said. "And I also do a lot of charity work that is rewarding. I am donating my time for that, plus I get to play some really nice [golf] courses."

Though his four Super Bowl rings are stashed in a safety deposit box, the games he played nearly two decades ago are as fresh in his mind as yesterday.

"I asked Al Davis during the latter part of my career if he thought I was a Raider even though I came from a different team," Hendricks said. "And he told me I'd be a Raider all my life."

Theodore (Ted) Paul Hendricks

Born November 1, 1947, at Guatamala City, Guatamala
Height: 6'7" Weight: 235
High School: Miami, FL, Hialeah.
Attended University of Miami (FL).

Established NFL record for most safeties, career (four).
Named as defensive end on *The Sporting News* College All-America Team, 1968.
Named to *The Sporting News* NFC All-Star Team, 1974.
Named to *The Sporting News* AFC All-Star Team, 1971.
Named to *The Sporting News* NFL All-Star Team, 1980.
Selected by Baltimore NFL in 2nd round (33rd player selected) of 1969 AFL-NFL draft.
Traded with a 2nd round draft choice by Baltimore Colts to Green Bay Packers for linebacker Tom MacLeod and an 8th round draft choice, August 13, 1974.
Played out option with Green Bay Packers and signed by Oakland Raiders, August 6, 1975; Packers received two first round draft choices (1976 and 1977) as compensation from Raiders, September 13, 1975.
Franchise transferred to Los Angeles, May 7, 1982.

			INTERCEPTIONS			
Year	Club	G.	No.	Yds.	Avg.	TD
1969	Baltimore NFL	14			None	
1970	Baltimore NFL	14	1	31	31.0	0
1971	Baltimore NFL	14	5	70	14.0	0
1972	Baltimore NFL	14	2	13	6.5	0
1973	Baltimore NFL	14	3	33	11.0	0
1974	Green Bay NFL	14	5	74	14.8	0
1975	Oakland NFL	14	2	40	20.0	0
1976	Oakland NFL	14	1	9	9.0	0
1977	Oakland NFL	14			None	
1978	Oakland NFL	16	3	29	9.7	0
1979	Oakland NFL	16	1	23	23.0	1
1980	Oakland NFL	16	3	10	3.3	0
1981	Oakland NFL	16			None	
1982	Los Angeles Raiders NFL	9			None	
1983	Los Angeles Raiders NFL	16			None	
	Pro Totals—15 years	215	26	332	12.8	1

Additional pro statistics: Recovered one fumble for 31 yards and a touchdown, 1971; returned one kickoff for 80 yards and fumbled once, 1972; recovered four fumbles and returned a blocked punt two yards for a touchdown, 1973; credited with one safety, 1974 through 1977 and 1980; recovered one fumble, 1974, 1977, 1981, and 1983; recovered two fumbles, 1978; ran 12 yards with lateral on fumble recovery, 1979; recovered four fumbles for four yards, 1980; recovered one fumble for six yards, 1982.

Played in AFC Championship Game following 1970, 1971, 1974 through 1977, 1980, and 1983 seasons.
Played in NFL Championship Game following 1970, 1975, 1980, and 1983 seasons.
Played in Pro Bowl following 1971 through 1974 and 1980 through 1983 seasons.

WILLIE BROWN'S interception return of a FRAN TARKENTON pass during the Super Bowl

7

WILBROWN

Willie Brown

The Oakland Raiders' training complex sits adjacent to Oakland International Airport in an undistinguished business park across the street from a well-trampled public golf course. Depending on the wind direction, the Raiders' practice fields are engulfed either in the sweet aroma of cut grass from the golf course or the pungent smell of aircraft fuel wafting through the dark canvas-covered eight-foot-high fence that surrounds the Raiders practice to satisfy the secretive Raiders owner, Al Davis.

There are two entrances to the sleek, two-story Raiders complex. The main entrance of the building is framed with black-tinted windows, and in front is a pond with a silver sculpture standing in the water. Behind the pond is a flagpole bearing the silver and black Raiders flag. If not for the flag and an awning painted with the team's notorious eye-patched pirate logo, you'd think that perhaps you had stumbled into the headquarters of a prosperous insurance company. Enter through the front door and you're greeted by a friendly and attractive receptionist offering a seat in the lobby that gives way to the team's nondescript business offices.

But the real business of the Raiders is conducted in the rear of the building, where there is another reception area manned this day not by a courteous receptionist but by a crusty, silver-haired security guard dressed in Raiders shorts and T-shirt who isn't pleased at having to turn away from a television blaring a tired rerun of *Kojak* to help a visitor.

There are no plaques or monuments commemorating the Raiders' rich history lining the corridors. The only items hung on the foyer wall are an oversize color print of the Raiders' three Super Bowl rings and a print of the nondescript Oakland–Alameda Coliseum.

The first floor is the players' domain, with meeting rooms and a lounge area complete with black leather couches and silver-tinted carpeting, a pool table, a pinball machine, and a line of desks with phones for the players to conduct any personal business. Down the hall to the right are the weight room and locker rooms, adjacent to the practice fields to maximize security and privacy.

It's in the empty players' lounge that I meet Willie Brown to talk. It's an appropriate place, considering that although Brown has been a member of the Raiders coaching staff for nearly every year since he retired in 1978, he still carries a player's presence.

Though he is in his late fifties, Brown still walks with the ease and grace of an athlete. While Jack Tatum and George Atkinson were the sound and the fury of the Raiders' defensive backfield, Brown was the old pro who kept order among the mayhem occurring within the Raiders' defense.

"Jack and George were crazy, and I had to keep them in line," Brown said. "They were tough, tough players, but I wasn't as aggressive. As a cornerback, you can't be as aggressive as a safety, so I let those guys be the bad guys. I was the good guy in terms of keeping them out of trouble. I was more of an anticipator. I knew exactly where the receiver was going. I read routes and formations and waited for the receiver to get there."

There are a few lines wrinkling Brown's face and a pack of cigarettes protrudes from the pants pocket of his Raiders sweat suit, but the lasting image of Brown will be the famous NFL film clip of him intercepting a Fran Tarkenton pass in Super Bowl XI and sprinting down the sideline for a touchdown, the cameras capturing every stride of Brown's poetic gallop to glory in slow motion.

It was a crowning achievement for Brown, who simply wanted to be a teacher when he left Grambling College in 1962 armed with a degree in physical education.

Brown grew up in Yazoo City, Mississippi, the fourth of eight children. Segregation was the order of day back in small-town

Mississippi in the 1950s, and Brown went to all-black schools. In the seventh grade, he started playing on his high school's football team, eventually playing six years of high school football, while also running track and playing basketball.

"My father was a hardworking man; he worked for the city and before that he worked in a sawmill," Brown said. "Growing up in that small town, I went to an all-black school, but we played football against the white kids. We played against them during the week and we played over Thanksgiving, and some of those guys also went on to be stars in college."

He attracted interest from Jackson State and a few other small schools, but when Eddie Robinson came calling Brown was on his way to Grambling. As a tight end and linebacker, Brown played in relative obscurity. The forward pass wasn't yet a staple of Robinson's conservative offense, making Brown more of an extra lineman than anything else. When he graduated in 1963, he figured his football-playing days were over.

"I wasn't thinking about playing pro football," Brown said, his voice tinged with a buttery Mississippi accent. "My main concern was to find me a nice little high school and be a high school coach. I never particularly wanted to play pro football."

It took Brown 32 years after he left Grambling to reach his goal of coaching high school football—in 1994 he coached at Jordan High School in East Los Angeles.

In between were 16 years spent as the premier cornerback in the NFL and another 16 with the Raiders as a coach.

When he graduated from Grambling, no one could have predicted that Brown would end up in the Hall of Fame.

In an era when the NFL draft consisted of 20 rounds, Brown wasn't even selected. Instead, he signed his first professional contract as a free agent with the Houston Oilers for a $500 bonus and $10,000 in salary if he made the team.

When he got to Houston, the coaches had a surprise. They tried him out at defensive back, a position he'd never played in his life. So Brown figured that if he jammed receivers at the line of scrimmage, he'd make up for his lack of technique. It was the first time the bump-and-run technique was employed on defense, and it saved Brown's career.

"I didn't know anything about being a defensive back and I never had the experience of covering receivers, so I started the bump-and-run and they only caught one pass on me during the preseason," Brown said.

It wasn't enough to impress the Oilers organization, which opted to save the $10,000 by cutting him loose at the end of training camp. Brown insists the move had as much to do with his color as it did with his ability.

There were already two black players on the Oilers, and if he made the team, Brown said, he would have put the Oilers organization one player over the team's unspoken quota.

"They released me on the last cut, and people were saying it was because I was the third black guy on the team and that made me the oddball. But I thought I had the team made. I was the biggest and fastest player at that position."

After Brown had spent a few days back home, the Denver Broncos called and Brown caught on. He spent four years with the Broncos, making All-League in his second year.

In 1967, the Broncos traded him to the Raiders for defensive lineman Rex Mirich in what has to be one of the worst trades in NFL history.

"The [Broncos coaches] had never seen the bump and run and they wanted me to show them, so I taught the players and coaches how to do it," Brown said. "I wasn't activated until the seventh game when they finally let a couple of guys go and I started playing and came back the next year and that's when I made All-League. But I got traded after my fourth year. They labeled me a troublemaker because I was making All-League and wanted more money. I was upset at first, but after I talked to Al Davis and a number of black players on the Raiders, I knew I was going to the right place. When I got to the Raiders, they had a pretty good secondary and I was switching back and forth between safety and cornerback and I didn't want to play safety. Dave Grayson was All-Pro at cornerback, but he moved to safety and I started making All-League every year.

Willie Brown: still a Raider

Brown, already an All-League defensive back, prospered with the Raiders, serving as team captain for 10 consecutive years. He intercepted a pass in 16 straight NFL games and had 54 career interceptions, four coming in one game against the New York Jets in 1964, tying a pro football record. He shares the all-time Raiders interception record of 39 with Lester Hayes.

Brown was an All-Pro as a 36-year-old, playing a young man's position, and no matter whom the Raiders drafted to replace him, he'd always beat back the clock.

"They had in mind to replace me, but I didn't care how many they had, how many they drafted, or how many people were stacked up behind my position. It didn't bother me. I felt could play as long as I wanted to, and my main concern was to win, so I also worked with the young guys coming in so they'd be ready to play."

Brown's statistics made him an easy choice for football writers who voted to put him into the Hall of Fame in 1984 in his first year of eligibility. He, like his longtime teammate Jim Otto, was also named to the AFL-NFL 25-year All-Star Team.

After retiring as a player, Brown settled into the Raiders organization as a coach, but a rift with former Raiders coach Mike Shanahan drove him from the team.

"Shanahan wanted no part of me, and we didn't get along," Brown said.

Brown bolted from the then Los Angeles Raiders in 1991 to be an assistant coach for legendary Washington Redskins coach George Allen, who in his seventies had decided to help Long Beach State University develop a football program. Brown took over as head coach of the fledgling program after Allen died in 1991, but the university pulled the plug on the football program in 1993. By then Brown had earned his master's degree in education from Long Beach State and volunteered to coach at Jordan High School while still on Long Beach State's payroll.

But his high school coaching days were short-lived. In 1995, Davis again came calling and Brown moved back to Oakland to coach the Raiders cornerbacks and direct player development.

Brown, carrying his star-studded credentials, which included four NFC Pro Bowls, five AFL All-Star games, a Super Bowl ring, and NFL Hall of Fame membership, came back to the Raiders to try to duplicate a secondary similar to his own playing days.

He taught Mike Haynes, who went on to become a member of the NFL Hall of Fame, and he tutored Lester Hayes, who in the late 1970s and early 1980s was the Raiders All-Pro defensive back and is now tied with Brown for the all-time Raiders interception record.

Today, Brown is married to his second wife, Evonne, and has three grown children from an earlier marriage.

As we talk in the players' lounge, Brown is caught between the Raiders of old and the new NFL, where free agency and multimillion-dollar salaries have changed the nature of the game.

"We made less money and worked harder," he said. "Every Monday night we did things together, and every Saturday night we'd have dinner together and study film. Today, guys aren't here long enough. It's much harder to have what we had."

His former teammates still revere the dignified Brown. To them, he's not Brown, he's WilBrown, the 10-year defensive captain who was their coach on the field.

When the Raiders made Jack Tatum their number-one draft pick in 1971, the coaches assigned Brown as Tatum's roommate. The message was clear: Tatum was to learn from the old pro. Brown immediately took to Tatum, helping him make the transition from the college game to the pros. He'd also have Tatum cook for him during training camp to make sure the collegiate All-American Tatum knew his place. Brown, as captain, would keep the defensive backs on the field after practice, making sure everyone knew everybody else's assignments.

"I knew if I told Jack that I was going to jump a route, he'd cover for me. You got to the point where you knew everything about each other. We lived and died and ran the street together. A lot of guys were outcasts from other teams, and knowing that we were all misfits tied us all together. There was a trust. If Jack needed a right arm and my right arm would grow on Jack, I'd give it to him."

Brown's brotherhood mentality belies a certain amount of pride in living up to the Raider outlaw reputation. Intimidation was just as much a part of Brown's game as his keen sense of anticipation and finesse. At 6 feet 1 and 210 pounds, he could deliver just as much punishment as his more aggressive teammates.

"We were the bad boys, and we wanted to be that way. We wanted people to fear us, and we knew we could intimidate people by the way we played. We had a lot of fun going to bars and going through town raising hell. We didn't go out and beat nobody up too much, only once in a while when somebody would mess with us. In Oakland and San Francisco, or anywhere we went, it was 'Here they are, the tough guys,' which was true."

What the bad-boy reputation didn't show was how badly Brown—and the rest of the Raiders—wanted to win. Pride was one thing, but so was their playoff money. These were the days when the owners held all the leverage and Davis counted the playoff money as part of a player's salary.

"We did a lot of things off the field, but on the football field, it was all business—all business," Brown said, biting hard on the second reference. "If John [Madden] had us out there for three hours, we worked for three hours. If we were out for four hours, we worked for four hours. For me the ball games were easy. Our practices were tougher than the ball games themselves. Going against Fred Biletnikoff, Dave Casper, and Ken Stabler every day in practice made it very tough on us, and it carried over to the ball games. It was something that the public should have been able to see."

William (Willie) Ferdie Brown

Born December 2, 1940, at Yazoo City, MS
Height: 6′1″ Weight: 210
High School: Yazoo, MS, Taylor.
Received degree in health and physical education from Grambling College.

Tied AFL record for most interceptions, game, with four on November 15, 1964, against New York Jets.
Named to *The Sporting News* AFL All-Star Team, 1964–68 and 1969.
Named to *The Sporting News* AFC All-Star Team, 1970 through 1973.
Signed as free agent by Houston AFL, 1963.
Released by Houston AFL and signed as free agent by Denver AFL, August 1963.
Traded with quarterback Mickey Slaughter by Denver AFL to Oakland AFL for tackle Rex Mirich and draft choice, January 21, 1967.

			INTERCEPTIONS			
Year	Club	G.	No.	Yds.	Avg.	TD
1963	Denver AFL	8	1	0	0.0	0
1964	Denver AFL	14	9	140	15.6	0
1965	Denver AFL	14	2	18	9.0	0
1966	Denver AFL	14	3	37	12.3	0
1967	Oakland AFL	14	7	33	4.7	1
1968	Oakland AFL	14	2	27	13.5	1
1969	Oakland AFL	4	5	111	22.2	0
1970	Oakland NFL	9	3	0	0.0	0
1971	Oakland NFL	14	2	2	1.0	0
1972	Oakland NFL	14	4	26	6.5	0
1973	Oakland NFL	14	3	21	20.3	0
1974	Oakland NFL	9	1	31	31.0	0
1975	Oakland NFL	12	4	21	20.3	0
1976	Oakland NFL	14	3	25	8.3	0
1977	Oakland NFL	14	4	24	6.0	0
1978	Oakland NFL	13	1	0	0.0	0
Pro Totals—16 Years		205	54	472	8.7	2

Additional pro statistics: Returned three punts for 29 yards and three kickoffs for 70 yards, 1963; recovered two fumbles, 1967 and 1972.
Played in AFL All-Star Game following 1964, 1965, and 1967 through 1969 seasons.
Played in AFL Championship Game, 1967 through 1969.
Played in AFC Championship Game following 1970 and 1973 through 1977 seasons.
Played in AFL-NFL Championship Game following 1967 season.
Played in Pro Bowl following 1970 through 1973 seasons.
Played in NFL Championship Game following 1976 season.

JIM OTTO stands
alone in the rain.

8

DOUBLE 00

Jim Otto

Jim Otto is the last of the original Raiders still connected with the team, a carbon-steel specimen of a man who played for the Raiders from the time the team was created in 1960 until he retired in 1976.

Otto never missed a game at center as a Raider, an absolutely startling statistic considering the thousands of blocks thrown and ensuing pileups that invariably snap linemen's knees and elbows. Through it all, Otto played at what was even then considered a lightweight 250 pounds, a man so stubborn and so old school that he refused to listen to the screaming pains of his body telling him to sit.

"I was very physical and never cared how I came out of it," Otto said. "It was almost like being a kamikaze pilot, and I've been fortunate that I landed when my wheels were down."

In return for sacrificing his body for the Raiders, Otto got an invitation into the Pro Football Hall of Fame and 38 surgeries, 28 of them operations on his knees. His right knee has been replaced six times, the last time in 1998, which nearly cost him his life: an infection that began in the knee almost spread to his heart. The infection was so bad that Otto was forced to stay in bed for five months. Doctors removed the joint to allow for proper healing, forcing him into a wheelchair for months.

Today, Otto remains a loyal part of the Raiders organization; it's clear that he never played for money. The most he ever made as a player was $75,000, a figure that is probably the biggest bargain in football history, given the number of Pro Bowl appearances he made and the number of games he played.

"I never had a guaranteed contract," Otto said.

Whatever Al Davis offered is what Otto took in those days, but Davis is returning the favor by keeping him around as the team's director of special projects—or a fancy way of saying that Otto organizes team alumni gatherings and charity events while trying to boost the Raiders' image among the increasingly apathetic Oakland fan base.

His office hardly reflects a man who is the epitome of the Raiders' "Pride and Poise" and "Commitment to Excellence" slogans concocted by Davis. It's a drab, interior space with no windows that makes the room seem even smaller than it is. Only a painting on the back wall depicting a youthful-looking Otto crouched in a pass-blocking position and a black leather jacket with his famous oo number stenciled on the back give any indication of his Raider royalty.

Behind the neatly organized desk, Otto looks more like a benevolent corporate middle manager than a member of the Hall of Fame. He's wearing a neatly pressed white shirt and a tie patterned with sports caricatures, and his glasses hang from a gold chain draped around his neck. Despite his numerous knee replacements, Otto walks surprisingly well, a testament to advances in orthopedic surgery and his toughness.

When he talks, his voice is full of conviction and a distinct level of recklessness, traits that turned him into a perennial All-Star and today tips off a nearly obsessive drive to succeed.

Otto's football career began in Wausau, Wisconsin, a paper mill town in the central part of the state where the farmland meets the pine-filled northern woods. Otto, the second oldest of five siblings, grew up poor. Although he was cut from his freshman football team because he was too small, he went on to become an All-State player, earning 48 scholarship offers. But he still remembers the feeling of being cut. It still bothers him that the coaches thought he was too small, and it still bothers him that he was ridiculed by older players because he went to a Christian grade school. This is a man who can hold a serious grudge.

Otto chose to attend the University of Miami partly because of the weather and partly because he wanted to use a high-profile program as a springboard to a career as a professional football player.

"I wanted to play where I would play all kinds of football," he said. "At the time, Miami was an independent and we played in a lot of different conferences. The Southeast Conference had a lot of speed, the Atlantic Coast Conference was more blood and beer, and the Big Ten was for big tough guys, so I thought I'd be seen by a lot of different people."

As a harbinger of what was to come, Otto blew out his right knee three weeks into his freshman year. The following spring, he tore up the other knee.

He eventually became a starter, though knee injuries and his small size resulted in little interest from the NFL. It was a rejection that crushed Otto, who wanted nothing more than to play for the Green Bay Packers.

When the NFL draft rolled around in the spring of 1959, the Packers and the rest of the league ignored Otto, shattering his illusions of grandeur.

The problem was Otto's weight. He had played both center and linebacker in college, his weight hovering around 210 pounds.

"I was very reckless and loved to hit people, but I was hurt all the time and I was small. That's what the NFL saw. I was surprised and shocked and thought it was the end of the world. I saw all my dreams going down the tubes."

But Otto had a good sense of timing. The AFL held its first draft in 1959–1960, and much to his surprise, he was drafted by the Minneapolis franchise that later became the Raiders when the team was hastily formed after the Minneapolis franchise's investors backed out of the old AFL.

"I was notified by telegraph, and I had to ask where the heck Oakland was," Otto said.

His contract was for $8,000, with a $1,000 "advance," and though he was drafted as a linebacker, Otto begged his coaches to play him at center, figuring that he'd last longer in the league at that position.

Otto was named the Raiders' starting center in 1960, and nobody else held the job for the next 15 years. His weight was no longer an issue. By the end of his rookie year, Otto had gone from a 210-pound linebacker to a 248-pound center.

"I really started working hard and I got into high-protein supplements and started lifting weights, and there weren't too many guys lifting weights back then. I was just very immature physically. I didn't shave until I was 22 years old, so I knew I could get bigger, stronger, and faster. But I was blessed to play offense. I figured I would just play five years and then go back to Wausau."

The five years turned into 15, with Otto playing in 210 consecutive league games, the most ever by a Raider. If you count the preseason, playoff, and All-Star games, he played in a total of 310 games.

"I worked harder and harder each year, and I wanted to be the best center to have ever played. It wasn't for money. When I signed three one-year deals for $20,000 for 1966, 1967, and 1968, I thought I'd died and gone to heaven. Al had me for three years for $60,000, but I never pushed the Raiders a whole lot. I was faithful in many ways."

Otto, a true company man, also hawked season tickets on the side for the early Raiders teams.

For the first three years, Otto would drive back to Wausau at season's end and spend the winters tending goal for the town's semipro hockey team.

Then he married his wife, Sally, and fretted each off-season about his future, even though he was already a perennial All-Pro.

"I never stopped thinking about my life after football," he said. "We had to work. I got into the liquor-store business and I helped promote and run a country club. I worked for a local concrete company here locally and made $150 a week. I also sold Raiders season tickets when they were building the Coliseum in 1965 and in 1966. Al paid me in the off-season to do that, and I sold more season tickets than anybody."

One season bled into another, and the end for Otto came unceremoniously during training camp in 1976.

While driving the blocking sled, Otto snapped the bone graft in his surgically repaired knee.

"I felt my knee pop. What had happened was that the bone graft had let loose, but I kept practicing. Finally, Al and I met, and he said that if I retired I could become the team's business manager. I went home and talked to Sally, and we decided that I would retire."

His only request was that he end his career in the last preseason game, against the San Francisco 49ers. He wanted to go out against the 49ers, a team he still despises.

"In the early years we were looked down upon as the doormat, but in my tenure, we played them 11 times and they only beat us twice."

More than two decades after his playing career ended, Otto can still work up a good hate for their archrival, the 49ers.

"I take things personally, and if someone calls my wife a name, tears down my Christian belief, threatens my country, or makes fun of my football team, I'll go to war. So the 49ers were never any favorites of mine, and they still aren't."

When the 49ers game rolled around in late summer of 1976, Otto, as team captain, won the coin flip and opted for the Raiders to receive the kickoff. The first drive was Otto's last. The Raiders drove down the field in a 13-play scoring drive led by a maniacal center who knew it was his last time in uniform.

"I went in with both knees braced and I ran 13 plays, just about all running plays. I wanted to beat up the inside of the line for one last time. We went down the field, scored, and snapped the extra point. Then I came out and held my helmet in the air and waved to my wife and said, 'That's all, baby, I'm done.'"

It was a career of steady acomplishments, on both a personal and a team level. During his iron-man career, the Raiders won seven division championships. Otto was a perennial member of the old American Football All-League team from 1960 to 1969 and was named to the NFL Pro Bowl from 1970 to 1972.

But Otto never won a Super Bowl. He still believes the Raiders could have beaten the vaunted Green Bay Packers in Super Bowl

II in 1968, despite the fact that the Packers pummeled the Raiders, 33–14.

"I never felt that we were inferior whatsoever," he said. "In Super Bowl II, we made a few mistakes like a dropped punt and they ended up with the victory, but I thought it was the year that we showed we were a power."

Otto has no great memories of his only Super Bowl appearance. The game's most vivid image isn't a block thrown, or the roar of the crowd at the Orange Bowl, where Otto starred years before at the University of Miami.

"We lost," he said. "I just remember chasing Herb Adderley after he intercepted a pass, and I remember trying to block Ray Nitschke and Henry Jordan. But I knew and felt that we were able to pass and run on the Packers. "

Even now, Otto can't name the player who gave him the most trouble on the field. "I played against so many players who are now in the Hall of Fame, like Dick Butkus, Willie Lanier, and Ray Nitschke, and they were all great. There were guys who were bigger and stronger than me, but when I played, I was the best center on the field. That's what motivated me to play, and I'd like to think that the players respected me."

After he retired in 1976, Otto spent two years as the team's business manager while building a series of businesses that eventually made him a millionaire. He owned liquor stores and five Burger King franchises, dabbled in real estate, and ran a prosperous walnut farm in northern California. He also recently retired from an ownership group that controls nine banks in northern California.

"In 1976, I took $175,000 in deferred salary and bought a 134-acre farm with 10,000 walnut trees. I had a manager running the ranch, and I used to leave Oakland after work and visit with my manager and make believe like I knew what I was doing. But I found out that you could depreciate walnut trees, and I made a fortune out of them," Otto said.

Though he left the Raiders and Oakland in 1977, Otto still kept in touch with Al Davis.

"When I moved to the country, Al called it a sabbatical. I'd come down on Fridays to be around for the weekend."

Jim Otto in his office at the Raiders headquarters.

For almost 20 years, Otto's business interests prospered, and in 1994, Otto was part of a failed effort to bring the Raiders to Sacramento. The group lacked enough cash to lure Davis, but in 1995, when the team moved back to Oakland, Davis brought Otto back into the fold.

"I do anything and everything. I do a lot of work with charities and do a lot of speaking on behalf of the team."

He also plays an important role for former Raiders who are struggling, quietly helping those in need. He is the link between the generations, stepping in to help arrange a substance-abuse program for one former player while offering financial advice to another.

Otto was so committed to the Raiders that he lived in a hotel in Oakland during the season, making the 135-mile drive back to his home in Auburn, California, twice a week to be with his wife.

It's hardly the life of a millionaire, but Otto can't seem to stop being a Raider or to say no to Davis.

"I've always went along with the program, and that's why I've been a Raider for almost 40 years. I was the last original Raider to play with the team, and I really took to heart what my coaches said. There were times when I was bashed and bloodied and I never left the field. I was the rah-rah guy and kept everything going."

Though Otto has managed to parlay the money he made as a player into a comfortable retirement, he can only imagine what he would be making if he played in today's NFL. And he has no doubts that he could have had the same level of success if he played in today's era.

He went into each game he played with a simple rule: to be the best center on the field. It's as if he almost willed that to happen, regardless of his injuries or the early, downtrodden Raiders days.

Whether it was raising walnut trees, selling concrete, or blocking linebackers, Otto's approach was one-dimensional, with total devotion to the effort. Somewhere in the depths of his mind, Otto was driven by the fear of failure. It's as if the voices of childhood insults hurled his way still echo in his head, driving him to succeed at almost any cost, and because of that you get the sense that Otto could still find a way to step onto a football field and dominate the line of scrimmage.

"The only difference from when I played and today is that I'd be a helluva lot richer," he said.

Not surprisingly, Otto doesn't care too much for today's players, who become millionaires the minute they leave college. In his mind, they haven't sacrificed enough to earn their money.

"They want to be pampered and they look for someone to pat them on the back. A lot of kids today don't want the hard work, they want the hard cash, and some guys just can't make it after football because they've been doted all their lives. But I've been a working stiff all my life. I came from nothing and will go away as nothing."

James (Jim) Edwin Otto

Born January 5, 1938, at Wausau, WI
Height: 6′2″ Weight: 255
High School: Wausau, WI.
Received bachelor of science degree in education from University of Miami (FL) in 1960.

Established NFL record for most consecutive games, one club, lifetime, 210, 1960 through 1974.

Tied NFL record for most consecutive games played in, 210, 1960 through 1974.

Established AFL records for most games, lifetime, 140, and most consecutive games, lifetime, 140.

Named to AFL All-Star Team, 1960.

Named to *The Sporting News* AFL All-Star Teams, 1961 through 1969.

Named to *The Sporting News* AFC All-Star Team, 1970 through 1972.

Selected by Oakland in 1st selections of 1960 AFL draft.

Oakland AFL, 1960 through 1969; Oakland NFL, 1970 through 1974.

Games: 1960 (14), 1961 (14), 1962 (14), 1963 (14), 1964 (14), 1965 (14), 1966 (14), 1967 (14), 1968 (14), 1969 (14), 1970 (14), 1971 (14), 1972 (14), 1973 (14), 1974 (14).

Pro statistics: Recovered one fumble, 1966 and 1970; fumbled once for seven-yard loss, 1971; fumbled once and recovered one fumble for minus 15 yards, 1973.

Played in AFL All-Star Game following 1961 through 1969 seasons.

Played in Pro Bowl (NFL All-Star Game) following 1970 through 1972 seasons.

Played in AFL Championship Game, 1967 through 1969.

Played in AFL-NFL Championship Game following 1967 season.

Played in AFC Championship Game, 1973 and 1974.

JACK TATUM on the run

9

THE REVEREND

Jack Tatum

Jack Tatum hasn't made a tackle since he retired in 1979, but he still hears the echoes of criticism that came from his viciousness on the field.

Cheap, they called him. Dirty, too. And though Tatum says that it doesn't matter to him, it does.

Not in a loud, defiant sort of way of course, but in a deep-rooted manner that still seems to simmer just beneath Tatum's quiet demeanor.

Tatum was named to the All-Pro team in 1973, 1974, and 1975 and established himself among his peers as the toughest safety in the league and a good cover man. Though he tied or led the Raiders in interceptions for two seasons and has 37 career interceptions, he never got much respect, he said, because of his aggressiveness and intimidating style of play.

Coming out of Ohio State as the Raiders' first-round pick in 1971 as a three-time All-American, Tatum wasn't a fool. He knew what the Raiders expected and he knew how to deliver the goods.

For Tatum, the hit began in his powerful legs, the explosive energy eventually moving up through his back and finally to his tightly coiled upper body until he unleashed the fury on some receiver who thought twice about coming across the middle after he'd been leveled by him.

Hitting was what Tatum was paid to do, and it suited his sense of being on the field. He was good at it, and he had the mentality to go along with the physical skills.

"If a receiver caught a ball, I felt I was doing something wrong," Tatum said. "My thing was that I was the sheriff. If they want to catch a pass, then let them pay for it. That was the deal."

Wearing the silver-and-black uniform with the skull and crossbones only enhanced Tatum's menacing image, and after George Atkinson taught him how to use his arm as a hook to deliver lethal clothesline blows on the enemy, his infamous reputation reached new heights.

Tatum wrote a book in 1979 titled *They Call Me Assassin*, based upon his new nickname.

Despite the notoriety gained from the book and Tatum's propensity for delivering punishment on the football field, he wasn't known as The Assassin inside the locker room. Instead he was known as The Reverend—a quiet, confident, articulate, and smart player—and a good guy.

"Some of the guys still call me The Reverend," Tatum said when we met at a restaurant down the road from the Raiders' training complex. "I just went about things quietly and wanted to take care of business. But on the field, I was a different person."

Tatum barely tops six feet (he's listed at 6 feet 1), but coming out of Ohio State University, he was the Raiders' starting free safety the minute the Raiders drafted him as their number-one pick in 1971.

"My afro put me at 6 foot 3," Tatum said, smiling at the memories.

Tatum still has a hint of the old afro, although a bit of gray protrudes from underneath his Raiders baseball cap that he thoughtfully wore so I would be able to recognize him.

Dressed in jeans, boots, and a golf jacket, Tatum has a compactness that still stands out. He's got that V-shaped sloping-shoulder look of a professional athlete, but you really can't tell he played football until you get a look at his hands. Unlike his flashier teammate and buddy George Atkinson, Tatum doesn't wear his Super Bowl ring. But if he did, he might have a hard time slipping the ring over his battered fingers that serve as a reminder of his playing days.

Jack Tatum, the notoriously vicious hitter, lives quietly in the Bay Area.

He is so soft-spoken that it's hard to reconcile his reputation with his demeanor.

"Once I put that last piece of tape on, I changed," Tatum said, sipping an iced tea. "If somebody talked at me, I talked back, but I let my play do the talking."

The toughness came from his boyhood in the rough-and-tumble neighborhoods of Passaic, New Jersey.

His parents moved Jack and his two brothers and sisters up from North Carolina when Jack was in the second grade. Tatum's father was a welder and his mother was a domestic worker.

"We had seven in our family, but it always seemed like more, with so many cousins in the house," Tatum said. "We would have 7 people at dinner, or we'd have 12."

Money was tight, but Tatum's football stardom at Passaic High School had the recruiters flocking to the Tatum house, promising Jack a full ride to almost any school of his choice.

Ultimately he chose Syracuse University, where as a superstar fullback who had gained 1,000 yards a season in high school, he hoped to follow such stars as Ernie Davis. He was all set to sign a letter of intent when Woody Hayes walked into his mother's house.

"I had my mind made up to go to Syracuse, but Woody came and pretty much recruited my mother," Tatum said. "He talked to me for 10 minutes and then talked to her for two and a half hours, and when he left the house my mom said that she liked that Mr. Hayes. She liked that he had holes in his shoes. He fit right in."

Tatum was a little less impressed.

"I liked Woody, but he was just like all the others. With a little push from Mom, I was at Ohio State."

When Tatum arrived in Columbus, he was in for a surprise. Recruited as a running back, he soon realized that Coach Hayes's trick was to find the best athletes and then worry about who would play where.

"Everyone I met said they were a fullback, and I immediately realized that we had about 33 fullbacks on the team, including John Brockington, who was 230 pounds," Tatum said.

As a freshman, Tatum split time at running back, and in his sophomore year, he switched to defense, becoming a hard-hitting rover back, a hybrid position of safety, linebacker, and cornerback.

He dominated the defense on an Ohio State team that is still considered one of the best teams in college history.

"We lost two games in three years, including the Rose Bowl against Stanford. We had 16 players drafted from my class, including six first-round draft choices."

After his senior year, Tatum knew he was going to be a first-round pick, only he figured he'd be drafted by the Cleveland Browns.

But despite Tatum's stellar All-American collegiate career, the Cleveland coaches felt that he was too short to play. It was the Raiders who drafted him and without so much as a preliminary phone call.

"I never even heard from the Raiders," Tatum said.

His first introduction to owner Al Davis was a rude one.

After Tatum signed for a base salary of $22,000 with a $16,000 bonus, the Raiders brought him out to Oakland for two weeks of workouts before he played in the annual college All-Star Game in Chicago.

"I was supposed to be out there for a week, but they kept me for two," he said. "I had never even met Al, until one day they had me covering receivers and they were running us to death. There was one guy who had a comment for everything I did, and finally I said, 'Why don't you just shut the fuck up.' I couldn't figure out why everyone was laughing as I left the field but it was because it was Al who I was talking to."

Davis liked Tatum's attitude, and since defensive back Dave Grayson had retired, the safety job was Tatum's to lose.

"There was no question that I was going to play," Tatum said. "It actually seemed like a step backward compared to Ohio State, where we had about 10 trainers and 15 training tables, and when I got to Oakland there was only one trainer with two training tables. I was thinking, 'So this is it, this is pro ball.'"

From the moment Tatum arrived at Santa Rosa, the team accepted him. They put him in the same room with perennial All-Pro cornerback Willie Brown to push Tatum's learning curve. When Tatum met George Atkinson, the veteran defensive back introduced himself by giving Tatum the keys to his new Cadillac.

"I had been in Oakland for a week and ran into George, and he gave me his new Cadillac and said to bring it back when I was ready, so I kept it and when I left minicamp I just gave the keys to the Raiders people. I felt accepted from the beginning here."

Both men had the same attitude.

"We prided ourselves on being hitters, and it was something we just developed," Tatum said. "We felt we could outhit anyone. From the beginning I felt real comfortable. My thing was just 'show me what to do and leave me alone,' and that was one of Madden's things. I didn't want a coach standing over my shoulder, and that's how it worked out."

Left alone to his develop his own style, Tatum's reputation for fierce play grew around the league.

"I always wanted to make the big hit, and I was going to hurt you if I could. We were aware of the reputation, though a lot of it was perpetuated through the press. But we were going to hurt you one way or the other."

Then, on August 12, 1978, Tatum's reputation became national news.

During a preseason game against the New England Patriots, wide receiver Darryl Stingley ran a slant pattern and Tatum drew a bead on him with only one objective: to separate Stingley's body from the ball. Preseason game or not, Tatum still hit like it was the Super Bowl.

The legal but devastating blow broke Stingley's neck and left him a quadriplegic.

More than 20 years have passed, and Tatum is still defending himself over the infamous hit, which remains as clear as yesterday in his mind.

"It was a clean hit, and was just one of the things that happen in football," Tatum said. "He ran a slant pattern, and I always played it the same way. I let the corner take the ball, and I took out the receiver. I had hit a lot of people harder and always expected them to get up, but [Stingley] didn't. We didn't know he was paralyzed during the game, and after I found out, things got kind of weird."

Tatum never spoke directly to Stingley about the hit, never apologized face-to-face. He said he made the effort after the game but was turned away.

"We made some attempts but it never seemed to work out," Tatum said.

The tragedy has overshadowed any of Tatum's accomplishments on the field and left him a marked man.

Tatum downplays the hit, but it affected him profoundly, changing the way he played for most of that season.

"I felt unfairly singled out, and it is still going on to this day," he said. "I was blamed for the incident, and I'll never be in the Hall of Fame because of the hit and some of the other things with [former NFL commissioner Pete] Rozelle. But I don't worry about it, because other players knew I was a force. That's what really counts."

Tatum's reputation with the league office wasn't helped by his flaunting of the league's uniform code.

For years, Tatum cut the knees out of his pants and wore his own black knee pads, a violation that drew a fine each week. But he didn't care about the fine, because, Tatum said, Davis paid it every week just to defy Rozelle.

Tatum's name appears only once in the Raiders' record books—for returning a fumble 104 yards for a touchdown in a 1972 game against the Green Bay Packers—but the statistics don't begin to measure his career.

For such an easygoing guy off the field, Tatum always seemed to be in the middle of the tumult on the field. If there was a controversial play, it seemed to involve him.

Consider the "Immaculate Reception" play that lives in infamy among the Raiders and their fans. It's a play that sticks with Tatum as much as the hit on Stingley.

During the 1972 AFC playoff against the hated Pittsburgh Steelers in a cold and rainy Three Rivers Stadium, the Steelers scored when a Terry Bradshaw pass deflected off running back Frenchy Fuqua into the hands of Franco Harris, who sprinted for a game-winning touchdown.

As Fuqua reached for the pass, Tatum met him and the ball at the same time, forcing a deflection that the officials ruled hit Tatum first, allowing a second Steeler to legally catch the ball.

Only, Tatum still swears that he never touched the ball.

"I've watched films and still have never seen a film that showed I actually touched the ball, and that hurt worse than anything," Tatum said. "Losing the game hurt, but so did the actions of the referees. They went into the dugout and called upstairs and waited five minutes before calling a touchdown. That's what really bothers me. Why didn't they call a touchdown right away?"

The play thrilled a national television audience, but the Raiders never recovered and it cost them another shot at the Super Bowl.

"They said it was my deflection, but I've seen the films and I still can't tell," Tatum said. "I wish we could have played the Steelers 16 times a season. Those were always such great games."

Tatum also delivered the hit on Broncos running back Rob Lytle in the 1977 AFC championship game on the Raiders' two-yard line that knocked the ball loose, only to have the officials rule that the hit was not a fumble. It changed the course of the game and, as far as the Raiders are concerned, cost them another trip to the Super Bowl.

In 1979, John Madden retired as head coach, and his departure also signaled the end of Tatum's tumultuous career in Oakland.

When Tom Flores replaced Madden, Tatum could feel the winds of change blowing, and at the end of the season, he was traded to the Houston Oilers, joining former Raiders teammates Ken Stabler and Dave Casper. It was a premature trade, Tatum said, because he was still in the prime of his career.

"I was at the top of my game, though I had had two knee surgeries, but Flores wanted his guys," Tatum said. "But I had a lot of fun down in Houston with Snake and Dave Casper. I would have stayed in Houston for 10 years, but then Bum Phillips got fired and I lost the enthusiasm to play."

He returned to Oakland and ignored other offers, knowing in his mind that he was done.

"I was finally making around $150,000, but once I was out, I was out," he said.

He married his wife, Denise, after he retired from football and now spends a lot of time with his two young children while involved in some real estate deals, including a golf course project with former Raider Raymond Chester.

"Now I'm just Jack Tatum the dad, not Jack Tatum the player," he said.

And in true Raiders irony, Tatum, who once flagrantly ignored the league's uniform policy, now spends his Sundays during the football season at the Raiders game working for the league by making sure the NFL players adhere to the league's strict uniform code. He also makes sure that sponsors' logos are properly displayed on the field and on uniforms.

"The league sent me a Park Avenue blue blazer," Tatum said. "But once a Raider, always a Raider."

John (Jack) David Tatum

Born November 18, 1948, at Cherryville, NC
Height: 5'11" Weight: 205
High School: Passaic, NJ.
Attended Ohio State University.

Established NFL record for longest gain returning a fumble, 104 yards, Oakland vs. Green Bay, September 24, 1972.
Named cornerback on *The Sporting News* College All-America Team, 1969.
Named safety on *The Sporting News* College All-American Team for 1970.
Named to *The Sporting News* AFC All-Star Team, 1975 through 1977.
Selected by Oakland in 1st round of 1971 NFL draft.
Traded with 7th round picks in 1980 and 1981 draft by Oakland Raiders to Houston Oilers for running back Kenny King, April 30, 1980.
Released by Houston Oilers, May 28, 1981.

			INTERCEPTIONS			
Year	Club	G.	No.	Yds.	Avg.	TD
1971	Oakland NFL	14	4	136	34.0	0
1972	Oakland NFL	14	4	91	22.8	0
1973	Oakland NFL	13	1	26	26.0	0
1974	Oakland NFL	10	4	84	21.0	0
1975	Oakland NFL	13	4	67	16.8	0
1976	Oakland NFL	14	2	0	0.0	0
1977	Oakland NFL	11	6	146	24.3	0
1978	Oakland NFL	15	3	60	20.0	0
1979	Oakland NFL	16	2	26	13.0	0
1980	Houston NFL	16	7	100	14.3	0
	Pro Totals—9 Years	136	37	736	19.9	0

Additional pro statistics: Recovered two fumbles for 26 yards and fumbled once, 1971; recovered two fumbles for 104 yards and one touchdown and fumbled once, 1972; recovered two fumbles for 18 yards, 1973; recovered one fumble for 12 yards, 1974; fumbled once, 1975; recovered one fumble for 11 yards, 1977; recovered two fumbles for minus seven yards, 1980.

Played in Pro Bowl following 1973, 1974, and 1977 seasons.
Played in AFC Championship Game, 1973 through 1975.
Played in AFC Championship Game following 1973 through 1977 seasons.
Played in NFL Championship Game following 1976 season.

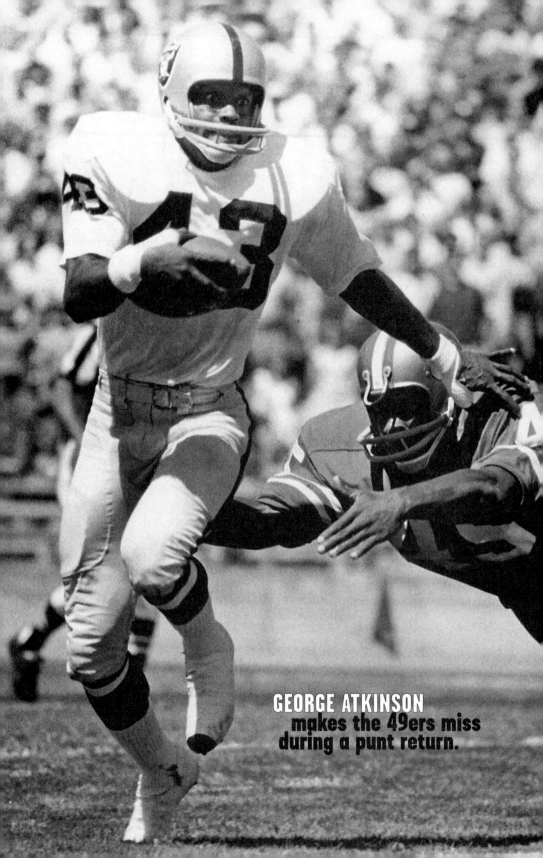

GEORGE ATKINSON makes the 49ers miss during a punt return.

10

THE HIT MAN

George Atkinson

Super Bowl XXXIII Sunday is 12 hours old and George Atkinson is sound asleep in a Ft. Lauderdale Marina Marriott hotel room, apparently still recovering from a very late night of NFL revelry. Atkinson, who lives in El Cerrito, California, just north of Oakland, was in south Florida taking a slice of the Super Bowl circus by representing the Raiders at the Taste of the NFL, a major fund-raiser trumpeted by the league.

When I called Atkinson ten minutes before our previously arranged noon meeting, the former defensive back was still in a slumber. A half hour later, he strolled into the lobby wearing black jeans, a black golf shirt, and dark sunglasses. On his left ring finger was his diamond-encrusted Super Bowl ring, and in his right hand was a lit cigar.

"Damn right I wear my ring. I earned it," Atkinson said.

Atkinson was an unheralded seventh-round draft choice in 1968 out of Morris Brown College in Atlanta, a typically chancy pick by Al Davis, who mined the small, relatively unknown black schools looking for players with speed, versatility, and toughness. More than 30 years after his rookie year, Atkinson's sprinter's build has given way to the effects of middle age, but he still has a sleekness about him as he strolls through the hotel lobby, completely ignoring the horde of well-heeled corporate types milling around before leaving for the stadium.

When I called Atkinson from the lobby, I suggested that we have coffee, but he turned down my offer, telling me that he doesn't touch the stuff. Instead, when we sat down in a far corner of the hotel's outdoor restaurant, he immediately ordered a Heineken and a side of extra crispy chicken wings. Somehow, drinking a beer for breakfast seemed appropriate for a retired Raider, especially for Atkinson, whose vicious reputation struck fear in the hearts of receivers who dared venture into his coverage area.

Paired with Jack Tatum in the Raiders' secondary, the two made a fierce tandem, drilling receivers with a seemingly calculated appetite for violence. At just 6 feet and 185 pounds, Atkinson was always one of the smallest safeties in the league, but his diminutive size, by NFL standards, never seemed to bother him. He was also a fearless kick returner who loathed the fair catch.

"I never, ever felt fear on the field," he said, answering my question as if I were completely out of my mind. "Jack tried to never let a receiver catch a ball, but I always liked to let them catch one ball early in the game just to let them know how it felt to get hit. But my attitude was that receivers were burglars breaking into my house and needed to be treated as such."

As a player, Atkinson liked to wrap his right arm from wrist to elbow in tape for use as a hook to deliver blows to the heads of receivers left defenseless while reaching to make a catch. His nickname: The Hit Man.

Today, that same wrist sports one of those WWJD bracelets that are supposed to help the wearer to live a holy life by reminding him of the message "What Would Jesus Do?"

Given the Raiders' reputation, it's an incongruous accessory on Atkinson, but at least the bracelet is in Raiders black. It's still hard to fathom that he would wear such a thing given his headhunting style as a player.

As we talked, it became clear that Atkinson has lived two lives: The first was a hard-living Raiders life. The second is as a bright, community service–minded motivational speaker who got his life together after spending a few years after retirement trying to figure out who he was.

"I never got into any real trouble, and when you look at my background, my troubles were as mild as anyone else's," he said. "I went to Catholic schools, and I came from a good family who instilled some morals and values."

Atkinson grew up in Savannah, Georgia, where he starred on the football and track teams at Johnson High School.

After graduating from high school, he went to Morris Brown College, a historically black school in Atlanta, where he continued to star on the football and track teams.

By his senior year, he had attracted the attention of Al Davis and other teams after being named an honorable-mention All-America football player while also winning three letters in track, once clocking a 9.6 100-yard dash. Fortunately for him, the Raiders were mining the small schools during the 1968 draft and made him their seventh pick. He was part of a strong draft for the Raiders in 1968, the second year of the combined AFL/NFL draft.

No longer were the two leagues fighting each other for players. Instead, the challenge for teams was to unearth players no one had heard of but who could contribute.

Along with Atkinson, the Raiders selected Ken Stabler, Art Shell, Marv Hubbard, and Charlie Smith in the 14-round 1968 draft. It was one of the most succcessful drafts in Raiders history; the players drafted would go on to make 15 Pro Bowl appearances among them.

"The AFL was looking for speed, and I could run a 4.3 40-yard dash," Atkinson said. "There was an acre of diamonds in those small schools."

Being a seventh-round pick made for little contract-bargaining leverage, and not long after the draft, Atkinson got his first introduction to Davis, who signed him for $17,000 along with a $7,000 bonus.

"Al is a master negotiator, and they had a pay structure for rookies," Atkinson said, laughing at the memory. "He wanted to sign me for $13,000 and a $4,000 bonus, and we haggled over that. Isn't that ridiculous?"

When Atkinson got to his first Raiders training camp in 1968, the Raiders were coming off a Super Bowl season and he was an unknown rookie. He was ignored by the veterans until he proved he was worth the bother.

"I was intimidated at first, because the Raiders had just played in the Super Bowl and the team was set. You had guys like Ben

Davidson, Dan Birdwell, and Ike Lassiter that were ass-kickers, and veterans didn't talk to you until you made the team."

During his first game, against the Buffalo Bills, Atkinson quickly made a loud statement to his teammates by setting a record with 205 yards gained in punt returns, including one for a touchdown. It was a good start to a great season for Atkinson, who was named AFL Defensive Rookie of the Year. Blending into the Raiders mix wasn't a problem for him.

"Madden had three rules that governed us: be on time, play like hell on Sunday, and don't drink in the hotel bars," he said. "There was no insubordination at all, though when Art Thoms came on a road trip dressed in farmer overalls and carrying a Snoopy lunch pail, John had to straighten him out."

The Raiders were so tight that they policed themselves.

"If a guy didn't fit the mold, then as players we'd cut him," Atkinson said. "There were guys who came to camp all cocky and didn't last three days. We made sure guys got along, and if there was too much trash talking, we'd game-plan them. You had to be tough mentally and physically fit to meet the Raiders standard."

After his rookie year, Atkinson established himself not only as one of the league's premier kick returners but also as one of the league's best defensive backs, aided by his famed head-hunting tackling that terrorized receivers. But there was more to his game than the clothesline tackle. He became a good cover man, his sprinter's speed allowing him to run with the best of the league's receivers. He still shares the Raiders' single-game interception record with five others after he picked off three passes against the Cleveland Browns in 1974. He retired with 30 interceptions, not far behind his teammate Willie Brown.

Madden and the rest of the coaches were amazed by the 185-pound safety who off the field looked like a schoolteacher but on the field went for the kill. It fit in perfectly with the Raiders' reputation for violence.

"I was an offensive player in college, but when you get to the pros, if you're not aggressive you get sent home," he said. "I was an attack-type ballplayer, and when Sunday came around, there was a transformation that had to take place."

Though Atkinson was matched up against perennial All-Stars such as Pittsburgh Steelers receiver Lynn Swann, Miami Dolphins superstar Paul Warfield, and Kansas City Chiefs receiver Otis Taylor, there are only two players who, he said, really gave him any problems on the field.

One was the strong-armed San Diego Chargers quarterback John Hadl, and the other was New York Jets receiver Don Maynard, who had a punishing running style.

"The toughest quarterback for me was Hadl," Atkinson said. "He could throw well and he knew how to look you off. He was tough. But for some reason, the guy I had the most trouble with was Maynard."

Atkinson was on the field for the famed "Immaculate Reception Game" against the Steelers and played in the infamous "Heidi Game" against the Jets in 1968.

But he is responsible for another fabled chapter of Raiders lore that is missing from official Raiders publications.

During the first game of the 1976 season, against the hated Steelers, Atkinson leveled Lynn Swann with a blind-side clothesline tackle that knocked Swann out cold. The Raiders went on to win the game, 31–28, with a last-minute score, but the real fireworks came after the game when an incensed Steelers head coach Chuck Noll called Atkinson part of the game's "criminal element." The hit also drew the attention of then NFL commissioner Pete Rozelle, who fined Atkinson $1,500, and the incident only fanned the flames of the already explosive rivalry between the two teams.

The Raiders went on to dominate the league the rest of the season, which culminated in a Super Bowl victory over the Minnesota Vikings, but Atkinson didn't forget Noll's comments. A few months later, he sued Noll for slander over his "criminal element" remark, charging that Noll's comment would tarnish his image, labeling him for life. To ease his pain, Atkinson wanted $2 million in damages. It was a classic case of the old Raiders us-against-the-world defiance so well orchestrated by Al Davis.

The case ended up before a jury in July 1977 in a two-week high-profile trial. The trial featured testimony by Raiders players defending Atkinson's play, and by Steelers players who painted Atkinson as one of the league's dirtiest players.

Like true Raiders, All-Pro guard Gene Upshaw told the court that Atkinson's hit was simply a part of football, and Raiders linebacker Phil Villapiano testified that he'd seen a lot worse hits.

In the end, the jury sided with Noll, and Atkinson is still offended.

"I hit Swann and they weren't pleased with it, and [Noll] came up with that criminal element shit. He directed it at me first, but he wanted to clean up other guys. I felt it was juvenile on his part and was uncalled for."

A few weeks after the trial ended, Atkinson went up to Santa Rosa for what would be his final training camp.

When Atkinson left the Raiders in 1978, he was only 31 years old, but he might as well have been 50. Though a brutal hitter, he took as much pounding as he gave, and his speed was the first of his skills to go. The Raiders' hard-living lifestyle didn't help much, either.

"Up until the last year, I didn't miss a game, so I was completely burned out and it was time to leave the game," Atkinson said. "The hits literally caught up with me, and mentally I just sort of lost it. Remember, I played five positions and I was on the field a lot."

After he left the Raiders, Atkinson spent a mop-up year with the Denver Broncos, then returned to the Bay Area without much direction. During his career as a Raider, he had bought into the liquor store business and he had some real estate, but it wasn't long before he was casting about, struggling to create a life after football.

"The transition for me was a tough one," he said. "All your life you are geared for one thing, and when you step out of the game it is tough. I had some liquor stores and some property, but I didn't know what I wanted to do and I was out there wavering. The game was over, and it took me four or five years to make the adjustment. You have to have an identity again and find out where your skills are. It should be easy, but it isn't."

In time, Atkinson went back to school, got his real estate license, and created some new opportunities for himself.

George Atkinson, a goodwill ambassador for the Raiders, soaks up the Super Bowl atmosphere

"When you have committed yourself to a profession and that profession is over and you have achieved just about everything you can, you have to refocus yourself, and that's the biggest challenge. As a player, you are in a programmed structure where everything is laid out for you by the team. Then you have to step out in the real world with no real agenda but your own. It's hard to dedicate yourself to a new identity. The most I ever made was $130,000, and that's per diem for these guys today."

Today, Atkinson is a motivational speaker at companies and schools. He is also a consultant to the Indian Gaming Commission.

About twice a month, Atkinson takes his motivational speaking program on the road, his second wife, Beverly, acting as his agent. Together, they have a nine-year-old daughter. Atkinson has two other grown children from a previous marriage.

Though he's weaned himself off his Raiders persona, Atkinson keeps close to the organization by doing some pregame and postgame broadcasting for the Raiders' local affiliate.

"I played in eight championship games, and the only regret I had was that we didn't win more Super Bowls," he said. "Shit, when we came to town it was lock up the goddamn kids and the dogs. We had the skull and crossbones on our helmets, the black jerseys, and the whole bit, and we lived it."

But now, after two decades away from the game, the self-professed "Hit Man" signs his autographs with a smiley face.

"Isn't that something," Atkinson said after politely signing for a group of fans from the next table. "Jack [Tatum once said] that a Raider shouldn't be signing his name with a happy face, but I do. People do change, I guess."

George Henry Atkinson

Born January 4, 1947, at Savannah, GA
Height: 6'0" Weight: 185
High School: Savannah, GA, Sol C. Johnson.
Attended Morris Brown College.

Established AFL record for most yards gained, game, punt returns, 205, September 15, 1968.
Selected by Oakland AFL in 7th round of 1968 AFL-NFL draft.
On injured reserve, December 6, 1977, through remainder of season.
Released by Oakland Raiders, August 3, 1978; signed as free agent by Denver Broncos, October 31, 1979.

Year	Club	INTERCEPTIONS					PUNT RETURNS				KICKOFF RET.				TOTAL		
		G.	No.	Yds.	Avg.	TD	No.	Yds.	Avg.	TD	No.	Yds.	Avg.	TD	TD	Pts.	F.
1968	Oakland AFL	14	4	66	16.5	1	*36	*490	13.6	*2	32	802	*25.1		3	18	7
1969	Oakland AFL	14	2	38	19.0	1	25	153	6.1	0	16	382	23.9	0	1	6	0
1970	Oakland NFL	14	3	35	11.7	0	4	12	3.0	0	23	574	25.0	0	0	0	0
1971	Oakland NFL	14	4	70	17.5	0	20	159	8.0	0			None		1	6	0
1972	Oakland NFL	14	4	37	9.3	0	10	33	3.3	0	3	75	25.0	0	0	0	2
1973	Oakland NFL	14	3	48	16.0	0	*41	336	8.2	1			None		2	12	1
1974	Oakland NFL	14	4	39	9.8	0	4	31	7.8	0			None		0	0	1
1975	Oakland NFL	14	4	77	19.3	0	8	33	4.1	0	2	60	30.0	0	0	0	1
1976	Oakland NFL	14		None					None				None		0	0	0
1977	Oakland NFL	12	2	38	19.0	0			None				None		0	0	0
1979	Denver NFL	6		None					None				None		0	0	0
AFL Totals—2 Yrs.		28	6	104	17.3	2	61	643	10.6	2	48	1184	24.7	0	4	24	7
NFL Totals—9 Yrs.		116	24	344	14.3	0	87	604	6.9	1	28	709	25.3	0	3	18	5
Pro Totals—11 Yrs.		144	30	448	14.9	2	148	1247	8.4	3	76	1893	24.9	0	7	42	12

Additional pro statistics: Recovered one fumble, 1970; recovered two fumbles for 26 yards and one touchdown, 1971; recovered two fumbles for 59 yards and one touchdown, 1973; recovered one fumble for eight yards, 1974; recovered three fumbles, 1975; recovered one fumble, 1977.

Played in AFL All-Star Game following 1968 and 1969 seasons.
Played in AFL Championship Game, 1968 and 1969.
Played in AFC Championship Game, 1973 through 1976.
Played in NFL Championship Game, 1976.

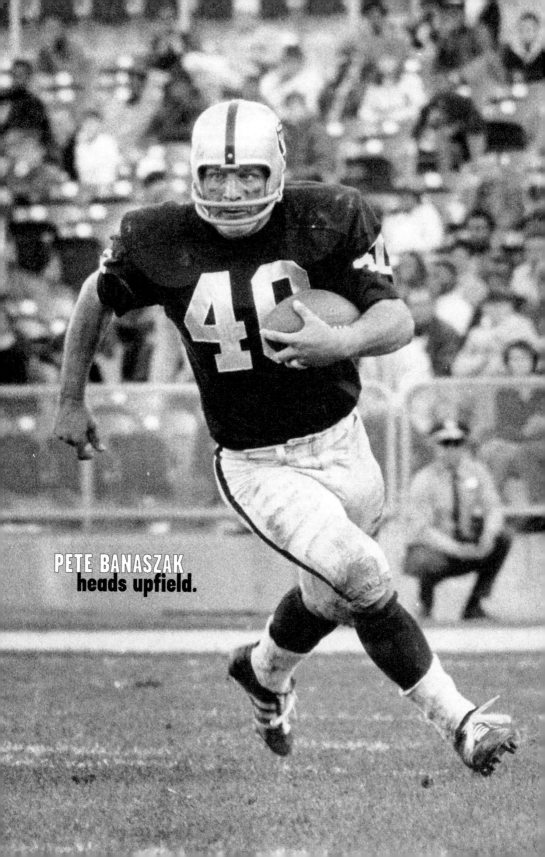

PETE BANASZAK
heads upfield.

11

THE ROOSTER

Pete Banaszak

In his 13-year Raiders career, Pete Banaszak ran the ball exactly like any parochial-school farm boy from Crivitz, Wisconsin, should: straight ahead, knees up, and God help the safety who filled the hole.

For Banaszak, flash did no good on the farm and it didn't do much good on the football field, either.

It's a rule that Banaszak still lives by, and damned if it hasn't taken him off the farm and into one of those gated country club communities with roads named after the natural habitat displaced by the homes.

Banaszak lives in Ponte Vedra Beach, Florida, the same town that serves as home to the PGA Tour. It's the kind of place where the locals are identified by a telltale characteristic: a tan line that stops just above the ankle where the leg meets the top of the golf shoe. After a steamy Florida summer filled with best-ball scrambles, member-guest outings, and club championships, the tan serves as a badge for the well-off. Banaszak earned his from a regular Sunday round with his wife, Sue, and the occasional loop with the boys at Marsh Landing Country Club, located about a stiff 3-iron from his house.

But you won't catch Banaszak in any country-club-crested blue blazer. His manner, utterly without pretense, is more bowling league than country club. In fact, if he weren't such a successful corporate executive, you'd think you'd run into the social committee chairman of the local Elks Club.

Banaszak is old school, which to him means inviting me down to his house on Saturday to talk, even though he traveled all week on business and even though he's probably got a million things to do, like changing the filter in his central-air unit, which is precisely what he's doing when I arrive.

But first, I had to get security clearance.

After a call to the Banaszak home from a kindly but properly suspicious guard alerting my arrival, Banaszak's wife Sue greeted me at the door and immediately offered me a drink to ward off the woolish blanket of the deep South's August humidity.

"Have a seat," Sue said. "And most of that Raiders stuff is all lies."

A couple of gulps of my drink later, Banaszak arrives, wearing the colors of his gloried past: a black polo shirt with the silver stitching touting a recent Raiders reunion, and a well-worn baseball cap sporting the logo of the University of Miami, his beloved alma mater.

Banaszak's 5-foot-11-inch, 210-pound halfback build has given way to a few too many business lunches, but the extra weight seems natural, because he's hardly a salad-for-lunch guy. His teammates called him "The Rooster" because of a stubborn cowlick. The name still fits, though his hair has turned mostly gray.

"Find the house all right?" Banaszak asked, even though his directions were Army officer precise. "C'mon, grab your drink and let's go into the living room to talk."

Furnished with formal furniture and well-napped carpet, the Banaszak living room is immaculate and looks as if a Banaszak has never set foot in the place. And within five minutes after we begin talking, Banaszak has abandoned the formality and hustled me into a den that holds the memories of his Raiders life.

On the shelves are his two Super Bowl rings, six hard-won game balls, and a host of framed pictures, plaques, and other assorted memorabilia. Prominently displayed is his battered Raiders helmet, left untouched from his last game, played against the Minnesota Vikings. On the floor is a box filled with scrapbooks that Sue compiled to preserve the memories.

The scrapbooks show a steady progression. There are yellowed clips of Pete as an unsure rookie. Pete pictured with his parents after the Raiders got trounced by the Green Bay Packers in Super Bowl II. And finally, Pete as a worn-out 34-year-old announcing his retirement.

In his 13-year career, Banaszak gained 3,767 yards on 964 carries. He scored 52 touchdowns with an average of 3.9 yards per carry, and he caught 121 passes for 1,022 yards. What the statistics don't show are the hundreds of holes he blasted open as he blocked for the faster backs and the hundreds of special-team tackles.

"I wanted to run kickoffs, I wanted to cover punts, and I wanted to be on a return team," Banaszak said. "I wanted to do everything. I think coaches today have got to kiss some ass just to get these guys to do something. Just because you're a starter and making $800,000, do you find it degrading to run down on a kickoff? That's the thrill of football. I used to love to run full speed and hit somebody instead of being hit. That was the greatest thrill there is. We used to win two games a year because of our special teams."

Only an occasional starter, Banaszak was famous for his insecurity. Even as a proven veteran, he'd sweat it out in training camp, fearing he'd be the next cut. His paranoia became a team joke, because whenever Ken Stabler needed three yards for a key first down, he'd call Banaszak's number, knowing that he'd find a seam.

"We each had our own job to do and we all did it well," Banaszak said. "I was a role player, goal line, short yardage, tough situations, like if we were backed up on our own 2-yard line. I would be in there until we got out around the 35 or 40 yard line. That was my role and that's what I took pride in. My greatest asset was that I was quick and could really get off the ball. I wasn't going to break a 75-yard run. That wasn't my role."

Banaszak's career can be summed up in Super Bowl XI. In the Raiders' 32–14 win over the Vikings, he rushed for a grand total of only 19 yards, but he scored on two short-yardage touchdowns to seal the Raiders' win.

Still, Banaszak worried constantly that he'd be cut. Each year in training camp as cutdown day approached, he would huddle with the team's beat writers, trying to figure out if he'd make the team.

As a fifth-round draft pick out of Miami in 1966, Banaszak signed a two-year deal that paid him $15,000 in his first year, $17,500 in his second year. It was the last multiyear contract he signed.

"I always signed year-to-year deals, so I thought I was always on borrowed time," he said. "I was always worried that I was going to be cut as sure as God made green apples. Funny that I ended up being a Raider as long as anybody."

Part of the reason for Banaszak's success can be found back in Crivitz, a town of 1,200 people that sits next to the Fox River, some 30 miles north of Green Bay.

Banaszak's dad was a dairy farmer who later sold oil for Shell Oil. Banaszak, his brother, and three sisters were raised with two rules: work hard and go to church on Sunday.

"I can remember Saturday nights with my mom shining our shoes and they'd all be lined up in a row for us to wear the next morning," Banaszak said, adding a kicker that flies in the face of the Raider image.

"I was raised in a strong Catholic family, and since I didn't know better, I was an altar boy for something like 16 years."

Banaszak was an All-State high school football star who drew interest from Miami thanks to a recommendation from former Miami Hurricane Jim Otto, who hailed from nearby Wausau and was by then already an All-Pro Raider.

Thanks to Otto's connection, Miami mined small-town Wisconsin for talent, and when Banaszak flew down to visit Coral Gables in February, his decision was made.

"My high school graduated 42 students, and I'll never forget my first visit. Here I was a real hick from the sticks, and I step off the plane and see all these palm trees and suntanned girls. I never knew a place like this existed."

Unheralded, Banaszak quickly adjusted from small-town Wisconsin to big-time football.

"My first two days in Miami I was scared stiff," he said. "We had some high school All-Americans from Pittsburgh and Cleveland, and here I am from the sticks and all. But when I saw them in uniform, I said to myself that they weren't any better than me. I had an inner thing that I knew that if I got the chance, I could play. I guess I felt I might be a little tougher."

After nearly transferring to Notre Dame, Banaszak started his sophomore year, gained 491 yards, and was given honorable-mention All-America honors. After his senior season, he was named the team's Most Valuable Player and then showcased himself in the North-South Shrine Game. In the spring of 1966, the Raiders made him their fifth-round pick.

His first year with the Raiders was a disappointment. He carried the ball just four times for 18 yards, casting some serious doubts on his future in pro football.

"My first year, I was just lost. I think I disappointed them a bit for a fifth-round pick."

He finally made his mark the following year, in 1967, with a huge game against the rival Kansas City Chiefs on Thanksgiving Day, gaining nearly 100 yards filling in for the injured Clem Daniels.

The Raiders went on to lose to the Packers in Super Bowl II, but Banaszak had established himself, his blue-collar approach helping him to settle in nicely with the Raiders.

"We always did things the hard way," he said. "We had to grind it out. While other teams would pick here and there, we'd take the ball and just bang away until we scored. We never knew how to play any other way."

Banaszak, like most of his other teammates, played just as hard off the field as on.

But his theory on the success of the Raiders is that for every flake on the team, there was a relatively sane player who balanced the load.

"I think I was one of the sane guys who held things together," Banaszak said. "Then we had guys like Marv Hubbard who once tried to dive off a bar into a shot glass. Or Ted Hendricks, who rode a horse around the practice field."

A training camp highlight, he said, was an annual visit by the local chapter of the Hell's Angels.

"They'd come up through Santa Rosa, and they'd always stop and we'd have a few drinks. Madden didn't mind as long as they stayed off the practice field."

The drinking may have wreaked havoc on the players' home lives, but it created a cohesiveness among the Raiders.

"There were certain buddies that everyone ran with, but we'd all end up at the same place. We'd get together at least three nights a week, and once a week we had what we called Camaraderie Night where everybody would go to a bar, not like today, where everybody runs off to do their own things. We didn't hold hands in the huddle or any of that other crap, but everybody believed in each other."

But as much as Banaszak liked to party, he also spent time thinking about his future off the field.

Thanks to a push by former teammate George Blanda, he got an off-season job working in sales for Crowley Transport, a West Coast–based shipping company. Part of his deal called for him to work out of San Francisco, and late in his playing career, he would put his time in with the Raiders while stopping in the office before and after practices.

"I'd bring my briefcase to practice and guys would be laughing, asking me if I carried a ham-and-cheese sandwich and all that," he said. "But it paid off. I mean there were times that in the off-season I wanted to get away from the guys. I loved them dearly, but I wanted to get away from people that only played football. I wanted to exercise my thoughts on something else. I really looked forward to the off-season and getting in front of one of our larger accounts and telling them why they should use us. It was a way of competing off the football field."

When Banaszak retired in May 1979, he fulfilled a pledge he had made to himself early in his career.

"I knew I'd come a long way from Crivitz, and I told myself that I'd never give them a chance to cut me. I would be the one who would say, 'Thanks a lot. I'm out of here.'"

Today, Banaszak is a vice president for Crowley, making considerably more than the $126,000 he made in his best year with the Raiders.

The typical week has him on the road, flying all over the country on business, handling clients.

"My golf clubs have more frequent-flier miles than I do," he said.

Banaszak's success hasn't gone unnoticed. Some of his former teammates who laughed at him for lugging his briefcase to practice have come to him asking for work. While he's disappointed that some of his former teammates have struggled since leaving the game, Banaszak's a realist.

"I don't feel sorry for any of these athletes that come out of football in distress. When you're a football player, you're given a chance to do what a lot of other people would kill to do. If you think a bit beyond, you can set yourself up by meeting the right people. I was fortunate, but God helps those who help themselves."

Part of Banaszak's post-career planning was investing in Technical Equities, a supposedly can't-miss investment company that catered to athletes, doctors, and lawyers.

The company turned out to be a fraud, and Banaszak, along with dozens of other athletes, was duped.

By 1986, Banaszak had lost upwards of $400,000, a hit harder than any blow delivered on the field.

"I mean, I trusted the guy and to have that happen, that hurt a lot," he said. "It was an expensive lesson, one that put a strain on my family. But I buried my head in my work to keep it off my mind, and I eventually got over it."

Though it's been 20 years since Banaszak left the Raiders, he keeps close to the game as a radio analyst for the Jacksonville Jaguars. Like many of his former teammates, he's not entirely pleased by today's NFL player.

"If you ask a player today what he wants out of football, he'd probably say $3 million instead of saying he wants to win a Super Bowl. But if it weren't for football, I'd be back in Crivitz worrying if I could get another cut of hay in the barn. I was taught that if you just work hard enough, good things will happen. That's why when I get home on Friday, I feel good, because I worked as hard as I know how. I've never wanted to do things just to get by."

Peter (Pete) Andrew Banaszak

Born May 21, 1944, at Crivitz, WI
Height: 6'0" Weight: 210
High School: Crivitz, WI.
Received bachelor of education degree from University of Miami (FL) in 1966.

Selected by Oakland in 5th round of 1966 AFL draft.
Released by Oakland Raiders, August 27, 1978; re-signed by Raiders, September 2, 1978.

Year	Club	G.	RUSHING Att.	Yds.	Avg.	TD	PASS RECEIVING P.C.	Yds.	Avg.	TD	TOTAL TD.	Pts.	F.
1966	Oakland AFL	14	4	18	4.5	0	1	11	11.0	0	0	0	0
1967	Oakland AFL	10	68	376	5.5	1	16	192	12.0	1	2	12	0
1968	Oakland AFL	13	91	362	4.0	4	15	182	12.1	1	5	30	6
1969	Oakland AFL	12	88	377	4.3	0	17	119	7.0	3	3	18	1
1970	Oakland NFL	10	21	75	3.6	2	1	2	2.0	0	2	12	1
1971	Oakland NFL	14	137	563	4.1	8	13	128	9.8	0	8	48	3
1972	Oakland NFL	14	30	138	4.6	1	9	63	7.0	0	1	6	1
1973	Oakland NFL	14	34	198	5.8	0	6	31	5.2	0	0	0	0
1974	Oakland NFL	14	80	272	3.4	5	9	64	7.1	0	5	30	1
1975	Oakland NFL	14	187	672	3.6	*16	10	64	6.4	0	16	96	1
1976	Oakland NFL	14	114	370	3.2	5	15	74	4.9	0	5	30	2
1977	Oakland NFL	14	67	214	3.2	5	2	14	7.0	0	5	30	2
1978	Oakland NFL	16	43	137	3.2	0	7	78	11.1	0	0	0	1
	Pro Totals—13 Years	173	964	3772	3.9	47	121	1022	8.4	5	52	312	19

Year	Club	KICKOFF RETURNS G.	No.	Yds.	Avg.	TD
1966–70	Oak. AFL-NFL	59			None	
1971	Oakland NFL	14	1	0	0.0	0
1972	Oakland NFL	14			None	
1973	Oakland NFL	14	3	48	16.0	0
1974	Oakland NFL	14	8	137	17.1	0
1975	Oakland NFL	14	2	24	12.0	0
1976	Oakland NFL	14	2	23	11.5	0
1977	Oakland NFL	14	7	119	17.0	0
1978	Oakland NFL	16	—	—	None	—
	Pro Totals—13 Years	173	23	351	15.3	0

Additional pro statistics: Threw one intercepted pass, 1968; recovered one fumble, 1970; recovered three fumbles, 1973; recovered one fumble for two yards, 1975; recovered one fumble, 1977.
  Played in AFL Championship Game, 1967 through 1969.
  Played in AFC Championship Game following 1970 and 1973 through 1977 seasons.
  Played in NFL Championship Game following 1967 and 1976 seasons.

MARK VAN EEGHEN blasts through the line.

12

THE COLGATE CONNECTION

Mark van Eeghen

The cabdriver eagerly tossed my bags into the trunk and sped from downtown Providence through neighborhoods lined with aging bungalows until we got to the outlying suburbs where Mark van Eeghen had agreed to meet me the following morning.

"Ever hear of Mark van Eeghen?" I asked the cabby, gauging if van Eeghen's football stardom in his hometown had held up since he retired in 1984.

"He's the Cranston boy who played for the Raiders, then the Patriots," the cabdriver said.

Coming up on the train from New York, I had a vision of quaint New England. Instead, I got the part of Rhode Island that feels like the inside of a body shop.

I had called van Eeghen a few days earlier to arrange our meeting, and he suggested we meet for breakfast, and when we met, he looked more like the prosperous insurance man that he is than the hard-driving 6-foot-2, 225-pound Raider running back who rushed for 6,651 yards and 37 touchdowns on more than 1,600 carries during his 10-year career, eight spent with the Raiders from 1974 to 1982.

Other than a few unnaturally bent fingers, there is no hint that van Eeghen ever played professional football. His memories of being a Raider are stashed away along with his two Super Bowl rings that lie in a safe-deposit box.

"I didn't go to Al Davis's or Art Shell's inductions into the Hall of Fame," he said. "I just got too busy. I'm not really part of the

Raiders family, and I don't have too much contact with the other guys. Football is over."

But it isn't really. Not when van Eeghen begins to talk about his career.

His father, a construction worker who spent lots of time away from home working on major projects in the Northeast, settled in Cranston without much of an interest in sports.

"There was no pressure for me to do anything, so I played everything," he said.

Though van Eeghen was an all-state running back at Cranston High West, the football factories ignored him. After some interest from the University of Rhode Island and the University of New Hampshire, van Eeghen decided on bookish Colgate University in Hamilton, New York.

"Football was two weeks of summer camp and a 10-game schedule. Then it was back to fraternity life," van Eeghen said.

A superstar at Colgate, van Eeghen was invited to play in the East-West Shrine Game after his senior year. During practice, he was a stranger among the scouts rating the All-Americans from the big schools. But Colgate was familiar territory for Al Davis. Davis had signed Raiders running back Marv Hubbard out of Colgate in 1968. In 1962, as a coach for the San Diego Chargers, Davis had drafted a running back out of Colgate named Jacque MacKinnon in the 33rd round.

As van Eeghen practiced during that rainy week in San Francisco, he caught Davis's attention. Other teams had expressed mild interest, but the Raiders never said a word to van Eeghen until his phone rang that spring day after Davis made him the Raiders' third-round draft pick.

"John Madden called that night, and I can't say he was the warmest guy on the phone. It was more of a declarative statement telling me I had been drafted, not a welcoming statement at all. But I was flabbergasted. I had absolutely no idea that Davis was watching me back in California. The Raiders never talked to me, never timed me, or anything else."

The day he was drafted, the Raiders put a puzzled van Eeghen on a plane to New York and stashed him in a hotel room as the rest of the draft continued.

The Raiders hardly rolled out the red carpet. Instead, they tried to pressure van Eeghen into signing a contract before any agents could foul up the deal.

"I was in a hotel room with some Raiders scouts and other people, and they laid something in front of me and tried to get me to sign, but I told then I wasn't ready. Basically, I got hustled to New York City for 25 minutes to sign."

Van Eeghen eventually signed a two-year deal with the Raiders for $30,000 his first year, $50,000 in the second year, along with a $50,000 signing bonus.

When training camp rolled around in July, van Eeghen thought he'd made a terrible mistake.

Because of a players' strike, the veterans were out of camp, leaving the rookies, free agents, and other fringe talent battling it out to impress the coaches.

"Every day was like a war on the field, and I fell into a mini-depression. But once the veterans came back into camp, things got a little easier. Madden rode the rookies hard, and I had a healthy fear of him. But when you're a rookie, until you've earned your spurs, you're a rookie."

Marv Hubbard, who was the Raiders' starting fullback, took van Eeghen under his wing and taught him what the coaches at Colgate didn't.

"Marv was a hard-nose like myself, and he was good to me. One of the first things he said to me was that I was the heir to his throne, and he taught me so many of the technical aspects of the game."

Van Eeghen's rookie year was spent mostly on the bench, watching Hubbard and Pete Banaszak get much of the work while van Eeghen learned about being a Raider.

"At Colgate, some of our best parties were after we lost," he said. "Coming out of a small school didn't help my confidence. I wasn't comfortable enough to let it all hang out on the field with so many guys coming from huge programs. But on the flip side, it helped me because everything was new and fresh to me."

With the free spirits spilling all over the Raiders' roster, van Eeghen preferred to stay in the shadows—always one of the boys, but still able to keep his distance.

"The wildness was overblown to a certain extent. The attitude was that if a rule had nothing to do with winning, then it wasn't a rule."

Van Eeghen also learned another difference between Colgate and Oakland after he separated his shoulder during his rookie year.

The common practice in the pros, van Eeghen said, was to amputate part of the clavicle to prevent future separations.

"The doctor kept telling me about how great legends like Willie Wood had taken the amputation route, so I figured if it was good enough for them, it was good enough for me. Funny thing is that I never separated that shoulder again."

After injuries forced Hubbard to retire, van Eeghen gained confidence and became a mainstay of the Raiders' offense. His smashmouth running style helped him put up some big numbers, including three consecutive 1,000-yard seasons from 1976 through 1978.

"As a Raiders back, you never took a play off. You either carried the ball or blocked at the point of attack."

Van Eeghen's biggest day as a pro came in 1978 when he rushed for 153 yards against the Green Bay Packers in Lambeau Field. The game, while helping catapult van Eeghen into the upper echelon of NFL running backs, also changed his approach to the spotlight.

Always his own worst critic, van Eeghen would evaluate his performance after each game, grading his play from blocks thrown to holes hit. It was a ritual to keep him from getting too satisfied with his performance.

"My goal was to hit every hole that the lineman would make; it was the least I could do to reward them," van Eeghen said.

But in the afterglow of the Green Bay game, van Eeghen told one of the newspaper's beat writers that in his mind, he had played the perfect game. The writer forgot to include the part about van Eeghen's self-criticism and the story ran with van Eeghen boasting about his perfect play, a notion that didn't sit all that well with his teammates and coaches.

"Compared to the others, I didn't use my leverage as a starter to spout off on things," van Eegehn said. "I just told the press what they wanted to hear. After the Green Bay game I stopped talking and the only other time I spoke out was when the team moved to Los Angeles."

He married his wife, Nancy, after his rookie year and their lives took on a certain rhythm. A month in training camp, five months in Oakland, then six back in Cranston. Eight years cruised by, and suddenly van Eeghen was an aging 30-year-old veteran with three young daughters and an increasingly uncertain football future.

The beginning of the end came in 1981, when van Eeghen no longer led the team in rushing after five consecutive seasons. The next season, the Raiders drafted Marcus Allen and van Eeghen became expendable.

During training camp, van Eeghen sensed his time was up. Just after he moved his family to Oakland for the season, he was waived, causing a bitterness that still remains.

"I didn't deserve that. The least they could have done was to tell me before I flew my family out," he said.

At the time, he was the Raiders' all-time leading rusher with 5,907 yards. Marcus Allen later shattered the mark with 8,545 yards.

Not wanting to let go, van Eeghen caught on with the New England Patriots for two unremarkable seasons and retired in 1984.

"The Patriots were 25 minutes from my house, so it made sense, but it was short-lived," he said. "It was obvious it was over.

"My approach had been that I was a football player for six months and then after the season I just hung out and had too much fun," van Eeghen said "It was just football until later in my career. You'd think it'd be easy for me to make the transition away from the game because professional football was thrust on me, it wasn't something I had planned on, but it didn't mean it wasn't a tough adjustment for me."

Instead of pressure to perform on the field, van Eeghen was soon consumed by a more serious pressure, this time from the Internal Revenue Service over a house-of-cards investment he made along with 100 other athletes, including former teammates Fred Biletnikoff, Dave Casper, and Pete Banaszak.

They were all supposed to make millions from investing in Technical Equities. Instead, they were all fleeced. Van Eeghen lost about $250,000 in the scam and saw his family's nest egg vanish.

"I might have gotten back 17 cents on the dollar," he said. "I was trying to have sums of money become available in the time of my life when I had to start over again. I wasn't tremendously hurt, but it does still affect me to this day. I had numerous battles with the IRS, and it was a 10-year debacle. But we didn't come close to jumping out of any windows."

Since he retired, van Eeghen has worked in the insurance business and is a district manager for the Andover Companies. He has three daughters in college, and his Raiders career is becoming a distant memory.

"All of my memories are of Oakland, but it's been so long that I'm beginning to forget that I even played. It's like it's not even me anymore. After all this time, I've realized that I can't fill the void that's left when you leave the game. Nothing can replace the rush of playing in a Super Bowl. Nothing in life can replace the feeling of 11 guys in the huddle during a last-minute drive. The thing is, you can't replace it, you just move on. It's taken me this long to figure that out, and now it's easier to live with myself."

Mark van Eeghen

Born April 19, 1952, at Cambridge, MA
Height: 6'2" Weight: 226
High School: Cranston, RI, West.
Received bachelor of arts degree in economics from Colgate University in 1974.

Selected by Oakland in 3rd round (75th player selected) of 1974 NFL draft.
On injured reserve with knee injury, November 21 through December 20, 1981; activated, December 21, 1981.
Franchise transferred to Los Angeles, May 7, 1982.
Released by Los Angeles Raiders, September 6, 1982; claimed on waivers by New England Patriots, September 7, 1982.

Year	Club	G.	Att.	Yds.	Avg.	TD	P.C.	Yds.	Avg.	TD	TD	Pts.	F.
		RUSHING					**PASS RECEIVING**				**TOTAL**		
1974	Oakland NFL	14	28	139	5.0	0	4	33	8.3	0	0	0	0
1975	Oakland NFL	14	136	597	4.4	2	12	42	3.5	1	3	18	5
1976	Oakland NFL	14	233	1012	4.3	3	17	173	10.2	0	3	18	3
1977	Oakland NFL	14	324	1273	3.9	7	15	135	9.0	0	7	42	4
1978	Oakland NFL	16	270	1080	4.0	9	27	291	10.8	0	10	60	5
1979	Oakland NFL	16	223	818	3.7	7	51	474	9.3	2	9	54	3
1980	Oakland NFL	16	222	838	3.8	5	29	259	8.9	0	5	30	3
1981	Oakland NFL	8	39	150	3.8	2	7	60	8.6	0	2	12	0
1982	New England NFL	9	82	386	4.7	0	2	14	7.0	1	1	6	2
1983	New England NFL	15	95	358	3.8	2	10	102	10.2	0	2	12	1
	Pro Totals—10 Years	136	1652	6651	4.0	37	174	1583	9.1	4	42	252	25

Additional pro statistics: Returned seven kickoffs for 112 yards, 1975; recovered one fumble, 1976, 1979, and 1983; recovered four fumbles for no yards and one touchdown, 1978.
    Played in AFC Championship Game following 1974 through 1977 and 1980 seasons.
    Played in NFL Championship Game following 1976 and 1980 seasons.
    Played in Pro Bowl following 1977 season.

One of the Raiders' smallest, but toughest, backs; CLARENCE DAVIS scores a touchdown.

13

CLARENCE DAVIS

High up in the Oakland hills on a winding little street is where Clarence Davis lives in Sunday-morning quiet.

It's a tidy house, modest, and like all the other houses in the neighborhood, built in the classic 1960s ranch style with stunning views of the city and the Bay. Up here, the gritty feel of Oakland fades into the coolness of the hills, a blue-green panorama where the sky meets the trees.

Davis, the undersized but locomotive-like former Raiders running back, bought the place early in his eight-year run with the team, a testament to his innate ability to take full advantage of the opportunity at hand.

Here, on this bucolic street running along the top of Oakland, things seem to make sense; you get a perspective of northern California's jagged geography. The city seems less intimidating, the people friendlier, the air clearer, and the sun brighter.

But the logic evaporates when Davis opens the door and introduces himself.

Dressed in white NFL Pro Bowl T-shirt and a pair of shorts, Davis is still built like a baby bull, with sloping shoulders, thick neck, and ropelike forearms dotted with scars from all the hits he absorbed during his career. There are just a few flecks of gray in his full head of hair and his mustache. But there's a faraway look in Davis's eyes, and his imposing physical appearance is immediately thrown off by his slurred speech and his shuffled step as his brain, ravaged by a series of strokes, struggles to put it all back together.

As a player, Davis stood only 5 feet 10 and weighed 205 pounds, but he had tremendous strength for a man his size, giving the impression that he was a lot bigger than he really was. He was as tough as he was strong, able to withstand the beatings he took from the much bigger linebackers and defensive linemen.

"You're early," Davis says to me, and he's right. I'm an hour early, but I impatiently knocked on Davis's door hoping it wouldn't be too much of an imposition.

Davis is hospitable enough anyway and leads me into his living room, which looks out over the Oakland Zoo and the rough neighborhoods of East Oakland. Far out in the distance is the Coliseum, sandwiched between ribbons of highway, the San Francisco Bay, and the mud flats of Alameda.

In the corner of the living room, next to the couch, is a three-foot stack of scrapbooks. In the dining room, the table is set for a service of six, with Raiders coasters sitting under Raiders glasses and Raiders napkins on top of the plates.

In two corners of the dining room are glass cases displaying Davis's past.

His number 28 black home Raiders jersey hangs in one case, framed by Raiders photos and memorabilia. The other case holds his Raiders game helmet, and another helmet painted a bright blue with the number 22 sloppily painted on the side. It's the helmet he wore at USC, but the school's classic red has been obliterated with blue paint for a college All-Star game after his senior year at USC. The helmet is flimsy, seemingly better suited for a Pop Warner league than for the famed student body right sweep.

With the table set and the scrapbooks pulled out of the closet and neatly stacked, it's clear that Davis, who lives with his 70-year-old mother Maria, is prepared for a visitor.

But Maria is still at church, so it's me, Davis, and Janet, a friend who happens to be the sister of his doctor.

After a few minutes of small talk, Davis gets to the point.

"I asked my doctor if I was living wrong or something," Davis said, still asking himself why his central nervous system has betrayed him. "Who am I to blame for the strokes?"

His speech is slow, almost tortured, as the words struggle to come out.

It's as if Davis knows exactly what to say, only his brain won't let him. Every few minutes, he clears his throat with a guttural sound.

"Excuse me," he says after every time he clears his voice, though he needs no reason to be excused. He's unfailingly polite, and therapy has improved his speech and restored much of his brain's circuitry.

Only, he can't fill in some of the gaps of his football career.

As if he has to convince me of his exploits, Davis goes into the dining room and returns with a stack of yellowed papers.

His movements are slow, his steps tentative, and when he hands over the stack for me to examine, his actions are almost childlike in their gentleness.

In the stack are Davis's football letters he earned in high school, at East Los Angeles Junior College, and finally at USC, where he took his rightful place in USC's steady succession of superstar running backs in the late 1960s through the early 1970s. First it was Mike Garrett, then O. J. Simpson, then Davis, followed by Anthony Davis.

The scrapbooks tell the story that Davis can't recall, and page after page is pasted with old newspaper clips, including a faded Jim Murray column from the *Los Angeles Times* that compares Davis with O.J., claiming that Davis never got enough credit because he kept his mouth shut, unlike the flashier O.J.

The two backs have a history.

Davis went to East Los Angeles Junior College a few years after O.J. and broke his rushing records, then O.J., a Heisman Trophy winner, helped coach John McKay recruit Davis to USC.

"I was very surprised," Davis said, remembering O.J.'s calls. "There was the Heisman Trophy winner and USC wanted me."

Then Davis haltingly explains in detail the other schools that wanted him. He can recall being recruited by former University of Washington coach Jim Owens, who had lured former Raider Ben Davidson up to Seattle, then Davis tells of the interest expressed by University of Kansas head coach Pepper Rogers, who was looking for another Gale Sayers.

But there was no doubt where Davis was headed.

When Davis was 15, his mother shipped him out of the Bronx to Los Angeles. Maria, who years earlier had moved Davis and his two sisters to New York from Birmingham, didn't like the gangs, and when Davis was 15, she sent him west to live with her sister and her mother. Then she, too, moved out to Los Angeles with Clarence's two sisters.

At Washington High School, he developed into a speedy but strong running back who also played on the defensive line, despite that fact that he was only 5 feet 10 and weighed under 200 pounds. He also ran track.

"And I won the city shot-put championship against all the big guys," Davis said.

After he graduated, Davis went to junior college in 1968 for more seasoning, and after two years, he followed O. J. Simpson to USC.

"I had made my reputation in Los Angeles and everybody knew me," Davis said.

Making the transition from junior college to USC was of little concern for Davis, though he was replacing O. J. Simpson, who had won the Heisman Trophy in 1968.

"Carrying the ball, that was just a natural thing for me," Davis said. "And I didn't care about replacing O.J., though I knew he was a legend. I just wanted a chance to play in the Rose Bowl."

Davis got his chance in 1970, when he led the USC ground attack to the Rose Bowl, defeating Michigan, 10–3.

Playing in the Rose Bowl fulfilled Davis's college goal, but a more personal highlight came in 1970, when USC played Alabama in Birmingham, where Davis was born and still had some family.

While starring at East Los Angeles Junior College, Davis drew heavy interest from most of the nation's big programs, but not from Bear Bryant and the University of Alabama, which still didn't field the most racially integrated football program.

Davis took the snub personally, and he made the Crimson Tide pay for passing on him as USC beat Alabama, 42–21.

"It wasn't any type of southern revenge, but I wanted to prove myself. I wanted to show them what they lost by not recruiting me," said Davis, who led the Trojans in rushing for two years and was an All-American in 1969.

After his senior year at USC, Davis, like so many other Raiders players before him, was dumbfounded to learn he had been drafted by the Raiders.

He had been talking with the Rams and had been hoping he'd be able to remain a hometown hero.

Instead, he was taken in the fourth round by the Raiders, behind Jack Tatum, Phil Villapiano, and Warren Koegel.

In Santa Rosa, Davis wasted no time dispelling any doubts that he was too small to play. Though he was a small back, he earned his respect with his blocking ability. Though he had adequate speed, he surprised everyone with his deceptive strength and fearlessness when it came time to block a blitzing linebacker or to help a lineman with a double team.

"I saw that Upshaw and Shell were a lot bigger than any of the linemen I played with at USC and I showed them how much I liked to block," Davis said. "They said I was like a guard in the backfield and they called me Super Rookie, and the fact that they had faith in me gave me a lot of confidence."

Davis made the team behind Marv Hubbard and Pete Banaszak. In his rookie year he played mostly as a kick returner, but he was productive, returning 27 kicks with an average return of 27.2 yards, the second-highest such average in Raiders history.

In his nine-year Raiders career, Davis averaged 4.5 yards per carry and had five 100-yard games. His best regular-season game came on November 16, 1975, when he rushed for 120 yards against the Cleveland Browns.

The statistics are hardly those of a Hall of Fame career, but Davis proved to be a steady and clutch performer.

Though he had some of the worst hands on the team, a catch he made in 1974 remains one of the Raiders'—and the NFL's—most memorable plays in history.

It happened in the first round of the playoffs against the Miami Dolphins, then an NFL juggernaut that was gunning for its third consecutive Super Bowl win.

When the 11–3 Dolphins came to the Oakland Coliseum to play the 12–2 Raiders, the game was rightfully touted as being as big as the Super Bowl, only this game proved to be much more exciting than most Super Bowls.

Both the Raiders and the Dolphins had had dominating seasons, featuring balanced offenses and stingy defenses. The Dolphins had just come off two consecutive Super Bowl wins, while the Raiders were trying to dispel the team's growing reputation for losing key games.

The tone was set on the game's first play when Miami's Nat Moore shocked and then silenced the boisterous Raiders crowd with an 89-yard kickoff return.

The Raiders battled back immediately, scoring on a Ken Stabler–to–Charlie Smith 31-yard touchdown pass.

But it was in the game's fourth quarter when things got really interesting.

After a field goal gave the Dolphins a 19–14 lead, the Raiders got the ball at their own 17-yard line with 4:54 left to play. After an 11-yard completion to Fred Biletnikoff, Stabler struck again, this time with a bomb to Cliff Branch, who made a diving catch on the Dolphins' 27-yard line. But the Dolphins' defensive backs never bothered to touch Branch to end the play. Once Branch realized he hadn't been touched, he got up and scampered into the end zone, completing a 17-second, 83-yard touchdown drive that gave the Raiders a 21–19 lead.

Not to be undone, Dolphins All-Pro quarterback Bob Griese brought Miami right back, and just before the two-minute warning, the Dolphins scored on a 23-yard run by Benny Malone, who outran the Raiders' defense on a sweep.

Down 26–21 with two minutes left, the Raiders got the ball on their own 32 and Stabler went to work. Two passes to Biletnikoff drove the Raiders upfield, and after a six-yard gain by Davis that put the ball on the Dolphins' eight-yard line, the Raiders called their last time-out with 35 seconds left.

During the time-out, Madden and Stabler opted for a pass play to Biletnikoff, but the Dolphins were hardly surprised and threw double coverage at Biletnikoff.

Under heavy pressure, Stabler looked off Biletnikoff and threw a desperation pass into the end zone as he was being tackled.

As Stabler went down, Davis made the game-winning catch in the crowded end zone with Dolphins defenders hanging all over him.

The catch became known as the "Sea of Hands Play," and added yet another chapter to Raiders lore while making Davis an immediate fan favorite. It's one play Davis remembers as clear as yesterday.

"I should have negotiated my contract right after that game," Davis said. "I had wanted to make a good impression with the fans, but after that game, I knew that they liked me."

In 1976, the fans had even more reason to embrace Davis.

That year, the Raiders again dominated the NFL, posting a 13–1 record, with only a 48–17 loss to the New England Patriots, spoiling what could have been a perfect record.

The season opened up with a 31–28 win over the hated Pittsburgh Steelers, the game that sparked the George Atkinson slander lawsuit against Steelers head coach Chuck Noll for his "criminal element" charges.

That year, Davis and Mark van Eeghen shouldered the running game for the Steelers, while Stabler's aerial attack to Dave Casper and Fred Biletnikoff proved nearly unstoppable.

Once the season ended and the playoffs began, the questions mounted over the Raiders' ability to finally win big games.

But the Raiders silenced the critics by beating the Steelers in the AFC championship game, 24–7, for a long-awaited return trip to the Super Bowl against the Minnesota Vikings at the Rose Bowl.

The Raiders, and especially Davis, were ready.

Though van Eeghen was the Raiders' leading rusher for the season, gaining 1,012 yards, it was Davis who led the team in rushing that day.

After ripping off a 20-yard gain on the Raiders' first possession, Davis went on to gain 136 yards on 16 carries. Plagued by a torn-up left knee for the past three seasons, Davis chewed up the Vikings' storied Purple People Eater defense with runs of 20, 35,

18, and 16 yards and was the game's leading rusher as the Raiders destroyed the Vikings, 32–14.

It was Davis's best performance as a Raider, but it wasn't enough to win the game's Most Valuable Player Award, which instead went to Biletnikoff, who had four clutch receptions for 79 yards.

"I could have been the game's MVP, and I was disappointed, but I was happy for Fred," Davis said. "I just wished we would have won more Super Bowls."

As was true of so many of his former teammates, the Super Bowl was the pinnacle to Davis's career.

Despite his great strength, the hits eventually caught up with Davis, who hurt his knee early in the 1978 season and was placed on injured reserve for the rest of the year. It spelled the beginning of the end of his 13-year career, though like most other athletes Davis felt he could play longer. But what the coaches saw was an aging running back with a bad knee that would probably only get worse.

After playing two more seasons, Davis saw his knee continue to deteriorate, and in training camp in 1979, he was unceremoniously cut by new head coach Tom Flores, who that year had replaced John Madden.

"Flores didn't know if my knee was strong enough to take the pounding, so one day in camp, he called me into his office and that was it. I went back to my room, packed my bags, told my roommate Jack Tatum that it was over, and then I left."

Davis turned 30 years old that year, and leaving the game so suddenly left him blank.

"I missed all the camaraderie," Davis said. "I'm not a preacher, and everyone lives their own life, but we had a lot of fun in training camp. And I missed the screaming crowds and I missed the money. But I decided to stay in Oakland. I had earned my degree during the off-seasons at USC, and I went to work in computers."

With the transition made, Davis settled into his second life, working and still staying connected to the Raiders through player alumni outings and golf tournaments, and making an occasional road trip with the team.

But Davis left the game unfulfilled.

His career statistics show that he played in 173 games, carrying the ball 964 times for 3,722 yards for a rushing average of 3.9 yards per carry. He scored 52 touchdowns in his career but never gained more than 787 rushing yards in a single season. On the surface, his statistics aren't about to put him in the NFL Hall of Fame, but the NFL doesn't keep track of the number of bone-jarring blocks thrown by Davis that allowed other Raiders running backs to break free. Nor does the NFL have any official measure for toughness, a category that Davis would have surely led the team in.

"I didn't achieve what I should have," he said. "I wanted to make a greater impression and get to the Super Bowl one more time and wear another ring."

Time marched on for Davis, who had worked for a local health care company and the James River Company.

Then, in 1996, on a fateful trip to take his two young children back to St. Louis where their mother lives, Davis suffered the first of a series of strokes that have caused permanent damage.

"I had just taken my kids back after a visit, and I was at the airport, trying to get money out of a cash machine, but I couldn't remember how to do it and I couldn't get any money out of the machine," Davis said, his memory aided by his mother, who had joined us in the living room after returning from church.

Davis returned from St. Louis on his own after suffering the stroke, and managed to drive home, even though he couldn't move the right side of his body.

"He went to the hospital for a week, and for a while he couldn't remember anything," Maria said. "He'd just sit."

As his mother was explaining how she'd flown up from Los Angeles to care for her stricken son, Davis could no longer control his emotions, breaking out in sobs as his mother filled in the gaps of his lost memory.

One night, frustrated by her son's condition, Maria sat down and sifted through the scrapbooks, typing out a line for each of Davis's milestones.

There's a line for Davis's graduation from Washington High School, a line for when he was named All-State, a line for when he won an award from the local Jaycees, a line for when he won his scholarship to USC, a line for when he went to the Rose Bowl, and on it goes. It's a five-page time line of his life, and Maria would sit down with Davis and go over every item.

"The doctor told me it helped [bring back Clarence's] memory," Maria said. "I just prayed that he would have some of Clarence's memories restored."

Though Davis can drive and pretty much care for himself, his mother has no plans to leave her 50-year-old son.

While Davis is in reasonably good health, no one knows when he may suffer another stroke.

"The funny thing is that Clarence was never sick a day in his life and he was so tough," Maria said.

Today, Davis spends much of his time in therapy to improve his speech and his motor functions. The Raiders, he said, haven't forgotten.

"My wish is to be able to travel with the team again," Davis said. "And talking with the other players gives me confidence. They say that once a Raider, always a Raider, and me, I'm a Raider for life."

Clarence Eugene Davis

Born June 28, 1949, at Birmingham, AL
Height: 5′10″ Weight: 195
High School: Los Angeles, CA, Washington.
Attended East Los Angeles Junior College and University of Southern California.

Selected by Oakland in 4th round of 1971 NFL draft.
On injured reserve with knee injury, September 14 through remainder of 1978 season.

Year	Club	RUSHING					PASS RECEIVING				TOTAL		
		G.	Att.	Yds.	Avg.	TD.	P.C.	Yds.	Avg.	TD.	TD.	Pts.	F.
1971	Oakland NFL	14	54	321	5.9	2	15	97	6.5	0	2	12	2
1972	Oakland NFL	11	71	363	5.1	6	8	82	10.3	0	6	36	4
1973	Oakland NFL	14	116	609	5.3	4	7	76	10.9	0	4	24	5
1974	Oakland NFL	11	129	554	4.3	2	11	145	13.2	1	3	18	0
1975	Oakland NFL	11	112	486	4.3	4	11	126	11.5	1	5	30	4
1976	Oakland NFL	12	114	516	4.5	3	27	191	7.1	0	3	18	6
1977	Oakland NFL	14	194	787	4.1	5	16	124	7.8	0	5	30	0
1978	Oakland NFL	2	14	4	0.3	0	4	24	6.0	0	0	0	0
	Pro Totals—13 Years	89	804	3640	4.5	26	99	865	8.7	2	28	168	21

Year	Club	KICKOFF RETURNS				
		G.	No.	Yds.	Avg.	TD
1971	Oakland NFL	14	27	734	27.2	0
1972	Oakland NFL	11	18	464	25.8	0
1973	Oakland NFL	14	19	504	26.5	0
1974	Oakland NFL	11	3	107	35.7	0
1975	Oakland NFL	11	9	268	29.8	0
1976	Oakland NFL	12			None	
1977	Oakland NFL	14	3	63	21.0	0
1978	Oakland NFL	2			None	
	Pro Totals—8 Years	89	79	2140	27.1	0

Additional pro statistics: Recovered three fumbles, 1971; recovered two fumbles for minus four yards, 1972; recovered one fumble, 1973 and 1975.
Played in AFC Championship Game following 1973 through 1977 seasons.
Played in NFL Championship Game following 1976 season.

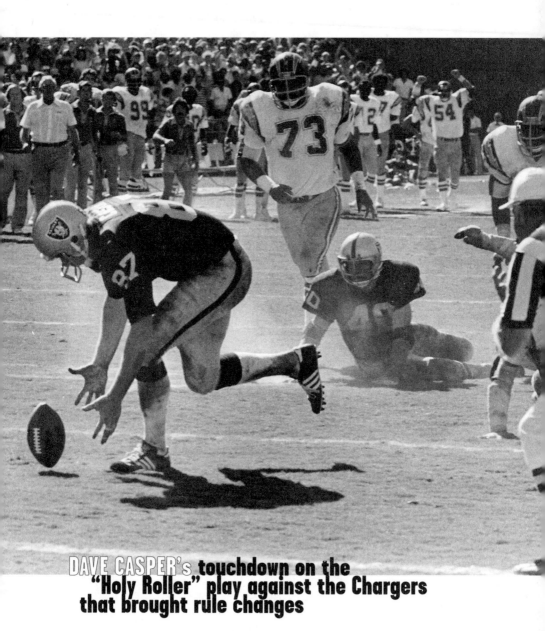

DAVE CASPER's **touchdown on the "Holy Roller"** play against the Chargers that brought rule changes

14

THE GHOST

Dave Casper

There are few signs of an NFL All-Pro career in Dave Casper's Edina, Minnesota, office, and that seems pretty much the way Casper wants it.

Instead of Raiders team pictures or other memorabilia hanging on the walls, there are plaques recognizing Casper as a member of the "Million Dollar Roundtable" and various other sales awards he's earned since he joined Northwestern Mutual Life after he retired from professional football in 1984.

On his desk are all kinds of reports with various numbers and graphs outlining investment planning, annuities, life insurance, and other financial products Casper sells to well-heeled clients. Even Casper's computer belies his Raiders legend status. When booting up, it sings the fight song of Notre Dame, his alma mater, not any Raiders message.

But on a bookshelf tucked away in the back of Casper's spacious office are three helmets that define his 12-year NFL career: his Raiders helmet, battered and chipped from years of banging into players; the helmet he wore during the Pro Bowl, the red AFC stickers beginning to peel away; and the helmet he wore with the Houston Oilers, where the Raiders traded Casper in the twilight of his career. The only piece of headgear missing is the helmet he wore for the Minnesota Vikings in 1983 before returning to the Raiders for a swan-song season in 1984.

The helmets would seem to be Casper's biggest calling card, but none seems to mean more to him than the others, and frankly, he seems just as excited talking about estate planning as he does reminiscing about Raiders memories.

He's a numbers guy, able to rattle off statistics from his career down to the tenth decimal, and he can recall specific yardage situations from games played 30 years ago.

He says stuff like: "The average score of my high school football team was 41.7 to nothing," the stats seemingly as fresh in his mind as if the game were played yesterday.

"What matters to me now is my business," he said. "I get up every day at six in the morning to run the numbers."

As Casper talks, he jumps from his desk to a computer that spits out reams of financial minutia, spelling out what it takes for a comfortable retirement. At the same time, he's fielding phone calls as he talks about his Raiders career.

"As the Snake says, I like to do three things at once," Casper said.

As a Raider, Casper had a reputation of being an intelligent but odd player. Then again, there weren't many academic All-Americans from Notre Dame on the Raiders.

"I'm always a little strange to people when they first meet me, but I'm fairly shy," he said. "People always thought I was different but I'm so down the middle that I'm unique. When I got to Oakland, I was a cowboy in a way, but I don't think I was weird. I may have been one of the strangest people out of Notre Dame, but I was one of the more normal guys on the Raiders. I liked to drink and I was a good Catholic kid, but I was not the kind of person to stand on celebrity and diplomacy."

Casper graduated from Notre Dame with honors in economics, and after spending 10 minutes with him, it's clear that he has a very agile and independent mind, characteristics that probably contributed to his reputation for driving some old-school coaches and players crazy.

Despite his laid-back look in jeans, a blue cotton shirt, and cowboy boots, there is a certain intensity surrounding him. He's blunt, honest, and opinionated.

Consider his take on his approach to football: "People would have called me a freethinker," Casper said. "At Notre Dame I was a captain, and I would bitch a little, but I never questioned anything. I played and drank too much and partied too much, but I was a good soldier.

"On the Raiders, I'd go to meetings and they'd tell me something once and I'd never make a big deal about anything, but I did have my arguments."

As a Raider, Casper was famous for his aversion to practice. He hated it, he said, because it was time spent trying to eliminate mistakes instead of learning to adjust to problems in game situations.

His theory was that practice made everyone too familiar with everybody else. Therefore, the timeless coach's credo of perfect practice was the least desirable result, because that meant there were no mistakes, or unknowns, that forced players to adjust. To Casper, making adjustments during a practice served a greater purpose than the endless repetition of typical practice methods.

"Dave was a smart guy and he was just bored by practice," John Madden said, getting no argument from Casper.

"I was a bad practice guy," Casper said. "What happens is that in practice, you can look as good as you want, but it really does you better if you pretend you don't know what is going on. Besides, it was not a good idea for me to line up and go full steam against my teammates. I am a totally different person when I get wound up."

Much of his distaste for practice can be traced back to Chilton High School in Chilton, Wisconsin, a farming town located near Madison, where his father ran a propane business.

As a high school senior in 1969, Casper was an All-State linebacker who led the team through a season that the folks back in Chilton still talk about.

"We were undefeated, untied, and unscored upon," Casper said. "And we only practiced for 75 minutes during the season. Most of the kids' families were dairy farmers and they had to get home from school to milk the cows."

As the youngest of three boys three years apart, Dave Casper didn't exactly have to live up to any family athletic standards. While he grew to be an agile 6-foot-4 All-State linebacker, his brothers were smaller and far less athletic.

"None of my brothers could catch and none could play sports," Casper said. "My father was only 5 foot 9, though my grandfather was 6 foot 2."

After graduating from high school, Casper accepted a scholarship to Notre Dame and played under legendary head coach Ara Parseghian.

Four years after leaving Chilton High, he was again part of an undefeated team, this time as captain of the 1973 Fighting Irish, which won the national championship with a win over Alabama in the Suger Bowl.

There was little glamour for Casper at Notre Dame, where he played most of his career as an offensive tackle. It was only after his junior year that Parseghian converted him to a tight end, and though he ended his college career with a national championship, he hardly enjoyed campus life.

"Notre Dame was hard and it wasn't much fun," he said. "But I was lucky to have played on some very good teams."

Casper was a wide-body tight end at Notre Dame who played a very physical game. Built like a lineman, he was a poweful blocker with decent speed and good hands.

While at Notre Dame, Casper played at 245 pounds and was slotted to be drafted by the Los Angeles Rams as a small but quick guard.

"I could have easily been 300 pounds, but I came out of school at 245 and played in the 230-pound range. I was one of the stronger tight ends at the time."

The scouts noticed.

"I was waiting around on draft day and there were three or four teams that were going to draft me. The Rams would have taken me as a guard, Pittsburgh would have taken me as a guard, and New England would have taken me as a linebacker. The Raiders were the only ones to take me as an end. I didn't care and I didn't know. I could have played offensive line, especially with the Steelers if they had put some steroids in me and bulked me up like everyone else."

In the spring of 1974, the Raiders made Casper their second-round pick after taking tackle Henry Lawrence in the first round, though Casper wasn't what you'd call a rabid Raiders fan.

"I just knew that they had neat uniforms and that was about it," he said.

Four days after graduating from Notre Dame, Casper got married and took off for Oakland.

His first day of training camp was a nightmare.

"I was tired and everything went wrong, and I popped a hamstring," he said. "Because it was the strike year, there weren't that many people in camp, and I didn't practice for three weeks."

"Other teams ran simpler routes. With the Vikings you never ran more than 20-yard patterns but with the Raiders you ran a lot of posts and corners. And the Raiders had a cadence problem at quarterback. Stabler would always nudge the center just before the snap of the ball because the quarterback always wanted the ball early, but it took me a year to figure that out because I was practicing with the second team quarterback."

The late start hurt Casper, and he spent his rookie year squarely on the bench.

"What happens is the second-team guys get paired with the second-team quarterback, and I got crummier and crummier because I developed bad habits. But my second year, I got healthier and I played on and off."

Casper first proved himself as a top special-teams player, though more by accident than by design.

Filling in for an injured member of the kickoff team, Casper flew down the field, shed some blocks, and made a great tackle, trapping the ballcarrier behind the 20-yard line and surprising everybody but himself.

"Madden was yelling, 'What the fuck was [I] doing in there?' but I was an All-State linebacker in high school and I could play defense, so after I ran down and made a solo tackle on the 17-yard line, it brought up the concept to the coaches that I could play."

Casper's big break came halfway through his second season in a game against the Pittsburgh Steelers when he finally cracked the starting lineup after replacing Bob Moore, who was injured.

"I came in and caught five passes in five minutes, and after that I just started," Casper said. "I went from sitting on the bench for two years to five years in the Pro Bowl."

While it may have taken Casper until his second year to establish himself, the Raiders' offense suited him well.

"The Raiders ran a more sophisticated offense than other teams, but it was still a running team first, and I was a blocker and always would be," he said. "The fact that I could catch a pass was all gravy."

From 1976 through 1978, Casper was the Raiders' leading receiver, averaging 55 catches in those three years for about 12.5 yards a catch.

"Snake didn't care who caught the ball," he said. "I was supposed to be in an area, and I got there rapidly. You just had to be at the right spot and make yourself available. And John Madden was a simple coach but always correct. Things were easy to execute, and I wished they would have allowed a few extra combinations. We really only had three or four running plays and four or five pass plays, and we'd run the same play one in four times. But Stabler was good at that. He was not a field general and he had no real concept of the game, but he had a presence that was great. Kenny called plays that didn't make any sense, but he made them work. He was not a dumb quarterback, but he didn't read the game plan."

Over time, the Stabler-Casper combination proved extremely effective, with Casper using his wide frame to create space for Stabler to throw between the linebackers and defensive backs.

Both made each other look good.

"Dave would go out and grab eight passes for 120 yards and then go drink, play his guitar, and fish," Stabler said of his old teammate. "Then he'd come in the huddle and start talking about what type fish he caught."

Perhaps the most famous Stabler-Casper connection occurred on Christmas Eve, 1977, against the Baltimore Colts in an AFC playoff game. The Raiders beat the Colts, 37–31, in double overtime when Stabler lofted a desperation pass to Casper in the end zone for the winning touchdown.

The game stands as the longest Raiders game in history, and the third longest in NFL history. For the Raiders it was a classic, going down in team history with the storied Heidi Game and the Immaculate Reception Game.

But Casper doesn't get caught up in what he used to be. Though he was an integral member of one of the NFL's notorious teams, Casper is detached from all the past glories. It's as if he could just as easily have taken football or left it entirely. After he retired, he stopped drinking, rediscovered his wife and kids, and made the transformation away from the game.

"I'm not one of those guys who has a lot fun," he said. "I drank too much and ran around and wasted a lot of time. In football, fun to me was when I wasn't injured. I would have just as much fun plowing a field as I would playing football."

After eight seasons, Casper had begun to wear out his welcome as a Raider, especially after the team began to fade in the late 1970s. But it wasn't a drop in performance that caused the Raiders to trade him to the Houston Oilers in 1980, it was his attitude.

"Any coach who was a good coach will tell you I was an exceptionally easy player to coach," Casper said. "I wouldn't make mental mistakes, but I would try something and make adjustments on the field. I was straightforward and there were a couple of coaches that had no reason to be coaches at all, let alone on the professional level. I've had some coaches who were so inept that they had to know that they were guessing. You'd sit in meetings and say 'why are you even bothering to talk to me?' I've had coaches who were helpful, but if a coach is five-foot-eight and never blocked a 240-pound linebacker or a 290-pound defensive end, I would use a different technique than they assumed would be used for some other skinny-ass tight end. I was a power blocker and a new coach would say 'Well, that's our technique' and I'd say, 'No, that's your technique.' But check with any running back. Van Eeghen led the NFL in rushing and when I was with Houston, Campbell led the NFL in rushing."

Like Stabler, Casper wasn't afraid to talk about his dissatisfaction with the organization. During a team meeting after the Raiders started out the season with a 3–3 record, Casper probably sealed his fate after singling out teammates who he felt were playing poorly.

"We were 3-and-3 and averaging 30 points on offense while giving up 30 points on defense, and we had a meeting with people saying that we had to play better as a team. I started saying, 'What the hell is this *we* stuff?' Gene Upshaw was playing like crap and other people were playing like shit, and I mentioned some names. I believed that you win as a team but lose as an individual, and you had to figure out what you did wrong. I said that there were things I was doing wrong, but I was sick of this *we* shit."

Shortly thereafter, Al Davis sent Casper packing to Houston, where he played for three seasons blocking for NFL great Earl Campbell. For an offensive-lineman-minded tight end like Casper, it was paradise.

"I was surprised when I got traded and the story was that they wanted to get rid of me because I was a pain in the ass," Casper said. "It wasn't a good training camp for me. I was working just once a day and I was still partying too much, and I was getting to be more cantankerous."

As for the Raiders, they went on to the Super Bowl that year with Raymond Chester at tight end in place of Casper.

"Houston needed a tight end and Ray Chester was a player, so the trade made sense," Casper said. "Personally, I had a great year and the Raiders went to the Super Bowl without me, but I enjoyed that year in Houston as an individual. I enjoyed the Houston people and I liked running the ball and blocking for Earl Campbell. The Raiders deal had gotten old."

Casper played two and a half years in Houston, then part of a year with the Vikings, and to prove there were no hard feelings, he finished his career with the Raiders in 1984.

"There were no problems with Al Davis as long as you didn't cross him," he said. "I just showed up and played, and I had one meeting with him in my life. Nobody knows Al. The players don't know him, and I don't think that even Al knows Al. But nobody ever screwed me. In fact, the Raiders probably had more regrets from the trouble I gave them."

Though Casper was away from the organization for only three years, there already were big differences under way. The Raiders, he said, somehow got their priorities mixed up.

"The Raiders were a good team first and a tough team second, and somewhere along the line, they got to be a tough team first and a good team second," he said. "When we played we had 43 great players and four projects. Now it's 35 projects and seven good players. You can have goofy guys on the field, but if you've got five or six goofy guys, then you get a critical mass. And while we had a couple of goofy guys, Willie Brown kept them in line. When we played, most of us were more normal than we appeared. The craziness was there because we didn't hide anything. Today, they put a fake covering on everything to make it look cool."

Like many of his teammates, Casper had trouble adjusting to life without football. After leaving the Raiders, he moved back to Minneapolis and bounced around a bit, first selling boats, then working for a Notre Dame alum. Finally, he began to sell insurance.

But he, too, was stung by investing his money in Technical Equities, the fraudulent investment company that fleeced dozens of professional athletes, including a handful of Casper's teammates.

"My life was not easy from 1986 to 1993," he said. "I sold my house and we went to work to retrench, especially after the Technical Equities deal."

Casper said his top salary as a football player was $140,000, but he wasn't making anywhere near that figure after he retired.

Today, Casper is successful enough to earn a six-figure income after working to build his book of business with Northwestern Mutual Life.

"I just made a decision to start at the bottom, but I'm known as a worker. I've got my German roots and I take a long-term approach. Anybody can sell to their brothers or sisters, but with most long-term jobs, there is a lot of rejection. I am an offensive lineman, and I know that very well."

With the separation from football now complete, Casper is more concerned about his clients than his playing days.

"I don't think about it that much," he said. "I have a connection with my teammates from what we went through, but little or none of my livelihood comes from the relationships with the Raiders. It comes from working my butt off. It is no different than being an offensive lineman. It's painful. People don't believe me when I tell them it's like missing a block, but [unlike football] at least it's not on film."

David (Dave) John Casper

Born September 26, 1951, at Bemidji, MN
Height: 6'4" Weight: 235
High School: Chilton, WI.
Received bachelor of arts degree in economics from University of Notre Dame in 1974.

Named to *The Sporting News* AFC All-Star Team, 1976 through 1978.
Selected by Oakland in 2nd round (45th player selected) of 1974 NFL draft.
Traded by Oakland Raiders to Houston Oilers for 1st and 2nd round picks in 1981 draft and 2nd round pick in 1982 draft, October 14, 1980.
Traded with quarterback Archie Manning by Houston Oilers to Minnesota Vikings for 2nd and 4th round picks in 1984 draft, September 20, 1983.
Released by Minnesota Vikings, July 20, 1984; signed as free agent by Los Angeles Raiders, July 25, 1984.
On injured reserve with foot injury, August 31 through November 2, 1984; activated, November 3, 1984.

		PASS RECEIVING				
Year	Club	G.	P.C.	Yds.	Avg.	TD
1971	Oakland NFL	14	4	136	34.0	0
1974	Oakland NFL	14	4	26	6.5	3
1975	Oakland NFL	14	5	71	14.2	1
1976	Oakland NFL	13	53	691	13.0	10
1977	Oakland NFL	14	48	584	12.2	6
1978	Oakland NFL	16	62	852	13.7	9
1979	Oakland NFL	15	57	771	13.5	3
1980	Oak.(6)-Hou.(10) NFL	16	56	796	14.2	4
1981	Houston NFL	16	33	572	17.3	8
1982	Houston NFL	9	33	573	15.9	6
1983	Hou.(3)-Min.(10) NFL	13	20	251	12.6	0
1984	Los Angeles Raiders NFL	7	4	29	7.3	2
	Pro Totals—11 Years	147	378	5216	13.8	52

Additional pro statistics: Recovered two fumbles and rushed once for five yards, 1976; fumbled once, 1977 through 1979 and 1982; recovered one fumble in end zone for a touchdown, rushed once for five yards and attempted one pass with no completions, 1978; recovered one fumble, 1979 and 1983; rushed twice for eight yards and fumbled three times, 1980; rushed twice for nine yards, 1982.

Played in AFC Championship Game following 1974 through 1977 seasons.
Played in NFL Championship Game following 1976 season.
Played in Pro Bowl following 1976 through 1980 seasons.

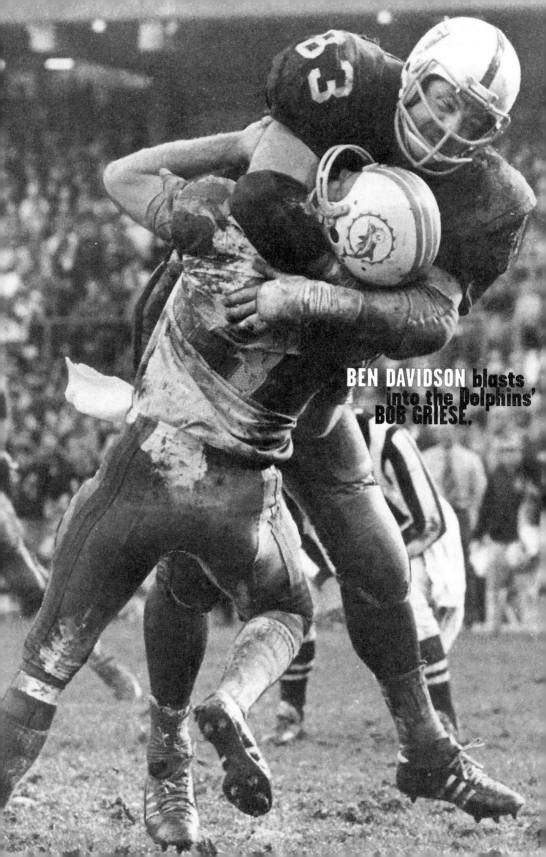

BEN DAVIDSON blasts into the Dolphins' BOB GRIESE.

15

GENTLE BEN

Ben Davidson

Ben Davidson spent his first years in football playing for the Washington Redskins for two horrendous seasons before being traded to the Raiders in 1964. I spent five years in Washington in a different life. So it was a homecoming of sorts for both of us when we met for breakfast in the Savoy Hotel in upper Georgetown.

Davidson, who lives in San Diego, was in Washington for his friend and former teammate Tom Keating's wedding. The two have a bond forged by spending six seasons playing three feet apart from each other, the massive 6-foot-8-inch, 275-pound Davidson lining up at defensive end while Keating played defensive tackle. Together, they dominated the Raiders defense that in 1967 set a record with 67 sacks for 666 yards in what was then a 14-game season.

Davidson's style was to rely on his massive size and a quickness rarely found in such a big man. As one of the league's biggest players, there wasn't a whole lot of finesse to his career with the Raiders, which began in 1964 and ended in 1971 with a knee injury. Then again, finesse was hardly a part of the Raiders' "11 Angry Men" defense that dominated the league with a swarming and aggressive style.

Consider that in 1969, the Raiders set the league record for most yards penalized with a whopping 1,274 in a season during which they lost just one game. Throw deep and hit hard was the secret to the Raiders' success in those years.

Davidson's most productive seasons in his 14-year career with Oakland were from 1967 to 1969. In each of those years, he was named to the AFL's All-League team as he dominated the defensive line while the Raiders dominated the AFL with a 37–4–1 record, including an appearance in Super Bowl II in 1967.

It's been a generation since Davidson retired, but he stills sports his signature handlebar mustache that enhanced his menacing look on the field.

When we met, he wore a khaki shirt, brown pants, and black boots, giving him the look of an aging but benevolent member of the Hell's Angels turned safari guide. Davidson played at 270 pounds, but he's nowhere near his playing weight now, thanks to a fitness regime anchored by bicycling.

"Hey, I'm 50 pounds lighter than when I played," he said, by-passing the bacon- and sausage-laden breakfast buffet for a mea-ger bowl of cornflakes in skim milk and sliced honeydew melon. Next to his oven-mitt hands, the cereal bowl looks like a teacup.

Davidson and his wife, Kathy, own two apartment properties in San Diego and he divides his time between collecting rent and trav-eling around the world, embracing his football ambassadorship.

"We have two rental complexes, one with 57 units, the other with 60 units, and the key is how much you keep," he said. "I was with the Packers in my rookie year in 1961, and our first rental property came after we won the NFL championship. The winners' share was $5,194.78, and we bought a triplex unit in Seattle with my father-in-law, who was a machinist for Boeing. We've been doing it ever since."

Davidson got his toughness from his father, a no-nonsense LAPD cop, but his gentle off-the-field demeanor comes from his mother, who was a library science major at the University of Montana. His parents met when his father, who had escaped rural Oklahoma for the Army, went into a bookstore in Butte, Montana, looking for a Pearl S. Buck book on the Orient. They married in 1938 and moved to Los Angeles.

"I grew up in East Los Angeles in a neighborhood that was eclectic, to say the least," Davidson said. "I started out in school with Jewish kids and ended up graduating with Mexican kids. I never played football in high school. I played basketball and was a pretty good hurdler."

Davidson was also smart. He graduated from high school as a 16-year-old and entered what was then East Los Angeles City College.

"I had a good background with books, and I skipped second grade along the way. I was big for my age, and I guess they wanted to get me away from the little girls."

Davidson's first taste of football didn't go well, as his junior college coach tried to run him off the team.

"He didn't want basketball players fouling up his football team, but I always thought I could play. I was always the enforcer in basketball, and I once fractured a guy's skull in a game. It was the early making of a defensive lineman."

Raw and unskilled, Davidson began to develop.

"I had only been to one high school football game, and my dad had taken me to see the Rams once. But in my first game someone hit me from behind and my hand landed on his face guard and I gouged my thumb into his eye socket. I thought to myself, 'I think I'm going to like this game.' Retribution was swift in football. It was right up my alley."

After two years of junior college, Davidson accepted a scholarship to the University of Washington for two reasons: Jim Owens, the coach, reminded him of his father, and his mother was from the Northwest.

"I had a few scholarship offers and the first plane flight I took was to Tucson to visit the University of Arizona," Davidson said. "I had good memories of Tijuana and I'd thought it would be exciting to go to the University of Arizona. They talked about driving down the road to Mexico and I thought that was exciting. But I had lunch with Jim Owens and I was very impressed. He talked about the program and the players and I thought he was a no-nonsense kind of guy. Plus, he paid for lunch and I thought that anyone who would buy me lunch was going to be all right I had been to Seattle, but only once, and it was a day it wasn't raining and I thought it was a beautiful city."

When the school mailed him his plane ticket, Davidson cashed it in and took the bus up to Seattle, stopping in San Francisco along the way, spending a few days hanging around the city during the heyday of the beat generation. When he got to Seattle, he was an 18-year-old junior.

"I fit into the program there even though I wasn't as competent as some of the other players. But I didn't whine and did what I was told. I worked my way up to second string my first year there as a junior and was honorable mention all-conference, which was strange as a second-string player."

Davidson became a starting defensive end and blocking tight end as a senior, and the Huskies played in the 1961 Rose Bowl, defeating the Wisconsin Badgers. That spring, Davidson discovered he had been drafted by the New York Giants by reading about it in the newspaper.

"Things were a lot less sophisticated then. When I got the paper I started at the bottom of the list, and when I got to the top 10 draft choices I figured I didn't even get drafted. I got up to the top five and I still wasn't there. Then I saw my name as a fourth-round draft choice of the New York Giants. I had no idea they were interested in me until I read about it. I thought I was going to go to the Dallas Cowboys."

Davidson couldn't make the Giants team out of training camp and was picked up by the Green Bay Packers for the 1961 season, a season in which the Packers won the NFL championship. For him, the win capped off an incredible year that began for him with an appearance in the Rose Bowl and ended with him playing for the Packers in the championship game. And on December 30 of that year, his oldest daughter was born.

His first professional football contract was for $9,000 with a $500 signing bonus. His agent, if you could call him that, was his pistol-toting father.

"My father went with me to sign, and he was packing a gun. I think it was the only intimidation thing we had going," Davidson recalled, laughing.

In 1962, Davidson was traded to the Washington Redskins, where he had trouble fitting into the organization.

When he arrived in Washington, the coaches told him he couldn't weigh more than 260 pounds. After one unscheduled weigh-in, he tipped the scales at 270, prompting the Redskins to cut him.

"The Redskins were obsessive about a player's weight," he said. "It didn't matter if we won or lost, it mattered what we weighed. One night I had a big dinner and got on the scale the next day and went all the way up to 270. That's when the Redskins fired me. Then Oakland picked me up and Al Davis said he wanted me at 300 pounds. So I got one team telling me to lose weight, the other telling me to gain weight, and I'm thinking that these guys are goofier than I thought."

When Davidson got to the Raiders in 1964, the team was only in its fourth year of existence—and it showed.

"Al was very organized, but otherwise, things were pretty low-budget. The Raiders' ticket office was in a converted gas station and the team offices were in one or two rooms of a hotel. My first night there I slept on a fold-away bed six feet long. The locker room was a metal building with four showers and the big guys got to shower first. It was showering of the fittest. I said to myself, 'What did I get myself into?' "

Things improved quickly for Davidson.

Davis had made an impression on Davidson when Davidson was in junior college. Davis, then a line coach at the University of Southern California, couldn't convince Davidson to stay in Los Angeles but finally got him a few years later.

"I was his kind of guy, which meant I did what I was supposed to do with a certain kind of verve. I worked hard and paid attention, and that's what got me through football. In 18 years, I never [took a playoff] on the field."

Davidson, who couldn't seem to fit in anywhere else in the NFL, was a perfect fit with the Raiders.

"All I wanted was for them to just leave me alone and tell me which guy to hit. What we had on those teams was a great loyalty toward each other, and people don't realize it. We had a lot of guys making up for shortcomings through hard work."

For Davidson, the instructions were fairly simple: hit the quarterback. And he followed the instructions to a tee.

The hit that brought Davidson the most notoriety was a head-snapping blow delivered to Joe Namath in 1967 that ended up in

Life magazine, bringing even more national attention to Davidson and the Raiders.

"We had been beating on Joe pretty good throughout the years," Davidson said. "We had played in New York, and before the game, Joe had done some interviews calling us a dirty team and how we were trying to hurt him. The officials must have gotten to town early and read the papers, because Namath drew a couple of questionable penalties.

"We lost that game and it stuck in our craw, but nobody said a word. Then the Jets had to come to Oakland, and that's when Ike Lassiter, our left defensive end, hit Joe across the face with a beautiful shot that cracked his cheekbone. But Joe, much to his credit, was a tough guy and he stayed in the game, and later on it was my turn. I hit him under his chin and knocked his helmet off, and *Life* magazine got a good series of photos of the hit. Unfortunately, Joe didn't have the ball when I hit him."

The hit only added to Davidson's reputation for fierce play, but it was Lassiter who broke Namath's jaw, not Davidson.

"Poor Ike. To this day he thinks that if the press had only gotten that right, he would have been the one doing the Miller Lite commercials."

Davidson also found himself at the center of some unwanted attention in a 1970 game against the division rival Kansas City Chiefs when he speared Chiefs quarterback Len Dawson in the back.

The Raiders were down by a field goal deep into the fourth quarter with no time-outs remaining, when Dawson ran a bootleg toward Davidson, who figured that with the game pretty much over, he'd try to hurt Dawson so the Chiefs would lose the following week, helping the Raiders' playoff chances.

"We needed a touchdown to win and field goal to tie, so when Lenny rolled out, he tripped over a leg, and I figured if I could hurt him, we'd be back in first place next week, so I speared him and did a somersault over him."

Unfortunately, Davidson delivered the blow right in front of the Chiefs' bench, sparking a major brawl that stopped the game for 15 minutes.

"Otis Taylor grabbed me around the neck and I got one punch in, but then I was buried under a pile of Chiefs. My teammate Dan Connors was right there to help me, and somebody grabbed him and pulled his helmet off and kicked him four times in the head. But I was on the bottom and nothing happened to me."

Once things were sorted out, Davidson got a penalty for unnecessary roughness, but three Chiefs were ejected from the game.

"Order was restored and Lenny called another play and we held them. Then we took over and got a long pass completed and Blands [George Blanda] kicked a 42-yard field goal. We ended up tying the game and stayed in first place, and we went on to win some playoff money. I believe that it was my quick thinking that saved the day for the Raiders."

Davidson's style of play earned him a reputation for being somewhat of a cheap-shot artist, but he insists it was all overblown, though he said that he did try to hurt Bart Starr in Super Bowl II.

"Bart and I were friends, but I took at swing at him during the Super Bowl, calculating that if I hit him, he'd be out of the game. I swung and missed. But that was a fun game for me. I had more tackles than anyone, and I had a sack. One of the highlights was when Packers fullback Ben Wilson had already been tackled and I speared him in the chest and the ball popped loose. It was a half-second late, but it was a beautiful shot."

Despite such admissions, Davidson insists he wasn't a dirty player.

"I did a lot of late hitting, but if I was as bad as the press made me out to be, players on other teams would have taken care of me. I played 16 years before I had a major injury."

After spending his final season in the game on the injured reserve list, Davidson had little difficulty limping away from the Raiders in 1971. There was no post-NFL turmoil. No problems figuring out what to make of himself after he retired.

"My take is that I've never really even had a real job," he said. "Life is a series of adventures, and my playing career was just one of them. Actually, I never really got all that wrapped up in football. I always had a variety of interests, and I've always been proud that I've exploited things to the fullest."

Ben Davidson, one of the biggest Raiders, still standing tall

Like his acting career.

When Hollywood needed the stereotypical brute, Davidson would occasionally find work. He has five films to his credit, ranging from Robert Altman's *M*A*S*H* to the X-rated cult classic *Behind the Green Door*, in which he played a bartender, fully clothed.

Cushioned by his real estate holdings, Davidson, a geography major in college, spent chunks of his off-seasons traveling, dabbling in different cultures and satisfying his natural curiosity. There were motorcycle trips to Mexico ("I have an affinity for all things Mexican," he said), escapes to South America, and forays into Canada.

The trips satisfied more than his curiosity. They brought him a sense of freedom from the structured life of an NFL player that chafed at his natural sense of independence.

"I'd be in training camp trying to use a phone to check on business and I'd have to wait in line for a pay phone while a rookie talked to his mother," Davidson said. "I'd wanted to be able to use a telephone in my room like a grown-up. I'd always ask myself why the coaches would have to shine a flashlight in my face at eleven-thirty at night."

After the Raiders, Davidson fell into a new venture that even he couldn't have dreamed up for himself. The Miller Brewing Co. signed him as a spokesman for its high-profile Miller Lite advertising campaign. For the next few years, Davidson got paid to drink beer while traveling the world selling beer. Perfect.

"I had a charmed existence there. I got called by an agent in New York right after I retired, and I think I fit their profile of guys you wanted to sit with in a bar and talk. So I go from the Raiders to the Miller Lite team, drinking beers with the guys. I made more in several Januarys making Miller appearances than I made in my first two years in professional football—with a lot less exposure to injury."

As Davidson nears 60, fitness and travel are more on his mind than football. From a distance, the NFL today looks like a different game to Davidson, who knows that much of his no-holds-barred style of play wouldn't be allowed in today's more regulated league.

"Deacon Jones and I were watching a game and a guy got a penalty for a head slap and I said to Deacon, 'I couldn't play now, I couldn't get along with the things I did.' I was a stumbling, fall down, get up kind of player and today's players are such great athletes. I was a player that took a minimal amount of talent and exploited it."

In fact, if people didn't pay him to play the engaging former football star, he probably wouldn't have much to do with the game at all. But he knows that people love to hear the old Raiders stories, and Davidson's got his stories down pat, ready for the next celebrity football cruise. He'll wryly recount his journey through the NFL, pointing out the often-ridiculous nature of professional football.

Like the time one of his teammates on the Raiders had the audacity to ask for pancakes instead of steak and eggs for the pregame meal. Despite the fact that many Raiders players were famous for their rebellious natures, the request for pancakes sparked a firestorm of controversy that involved the hotel waitress, the players, and eventually John Madden, who didn't appreciate having to deal with a food crisis hours before a game.

He also recalls when Warren Wells invited a black minister to speak to his teammates before a game: "We had a black preacher come in, and Madden didn't know whether to tell the guy to get out or what to do, so consequently the preacher gets up and addresses the team, and it was real rabble-rousing stuff, like telling black guys to go out and loot and burn and other crazy stuff. When the thing is over, all the guys were kind of looking around and wondering how the other guys were taking it. So we go out to practice and the black guys are apologizing to the white guys and the white guys are apologizing to the black guys because no one wanted to think anyone was biased. On most other teams that preacher would have caused trouble, but we realized that we were above it and it wasn't going to affect us adversely. It was because we had good leadership. That was part of being on the Raiders."

But when he's off the celebrity clock, Davidson isn't all what his trademark handlebar mustache and gruff voice would suggest.

"I've always taken pride in the fact that I can fit in anywhere," he said. "I've met presidents and talked to them, and I've been in bars in tropical Mexico where workers would come in after work with machetes, and I can talk to them. Everyone thinks I'm a sports guy, but I've never paid much attention to that. I was an overgrown kid from Los Angeles and played a kid's game and got paid for it."

Benjamin Earl Davidson

Born June 14, 1940, at Los Angeles, CA
Height: 6'7" Weight: 275
High School: Los Angeles, CA, Woodrow Wilson.
Attended East Lost Angeles Junior College and University of Washington.

Named to *The Sporting News* AFL All-Star Team, 1967.
Selected by New York in 4th round of 1961 NFL draft.
Traded by New York NFL to Green Bay NFL for draft choice, 1961.
Traded by Green Bay NFL to Washington NFL for 5th round draft choice, 1962.
Released by Washington NFL; signed by Oakland AFL, 1964.
Green Bay NFL, 1961; Washington NFL, 1962 through 1963; Oakland AFL, 1964 through 1969; Oakland NFL, 1970 through 1971.
Games: 1961 (14), 1962 (14), 1963 (14), 1964 (12), 1965 (14), 1966 (14), 1967 (14), 1968 (14), 1969 (14), 1970 (14), 1971 (14).

Additional pro statistics: Recovered one fumble, 1971.
    Played in AFL All-Star Game following 1966 through 1968 seasons.
    Played in NFL Championship Game, 1961.
    Played in AFL Championship Game, 1967 through 1969.
    Played in AFL-NFL Championship Game following 1967 season.

Hall of Fame guard GENE UPSHAW leads the way for PETE BANASZAK.

16

THE GOVERNOR

Gene Upshaw

As a Raider, Gene Upshaw would dream about a political career, maybe even becoming the governor of California. He'd think about it, and maybe plan in his head how after he retired, he'd get into politics in California, first on a local level, then work his way up until he lived in the governor's mansion.

Upshaw wanted to have a voice, a say in what was happening around him, which was ironic considering that nobody is more invisible, more anonymous on a football field than an offensive lineman.

But Upshaw was different. He was a talker on the field and in the locker room. His teammates called him The Governor not just because of his political ambitions, but also because he talked all the time, a real clubhouse lawyer, driving some of his teammates crazy with his mouth, but still a natural leader.

So it was only right for the players to vote Upshaw as their union representative. He could talk, sure, but he was also a high-profile Raider who made All-Pro every year and had the ear of owner Al Davis.

His first year as a player representative was in 1970, his third year in the league. All of a sudden, Upshaw was a union man.

"When I first got to the Raiders, the veterans made me join the union. I figured that if I was going to pay the dues, which at the time cost $75, I wanted to know what was going on," said Upshaw, who traded in his political ambitions to become a labor leader.

What seemed impossible during Upshaw's glory years with the Raiders is now reality. A black former player with no law degree now helps control the fortunes of the richest professional sports league on the planet by virtue of his job as executive director of the National Football League Players Association.

To today's NFL players who make a minimum of $250,000 a year and have the luxury of free agency, a pension, and the rights to millions of dollars of NFL merchandise sales, Upshaw's a regular Joe Hill.

To the power brokers at the league's Park Avenue offices, Upshaw is more partner than adversary, the guy they can't control because he has played the game better than just about anyone else and he can walk into any NFL locker room and understand. He's even testified on Capitol Hill with NFL commissioner Paul Tagliabue, both of them sitting French cuff to French cuff taking the same side on antitrust issues and other concerns related to the league.

To his former teammates, Upshaw may sit in a high-powered office with a fancy downtown D.C. address, but he's still a Raider. Always will be, too.

"It's just the way it is," Upshaw said. "It's something about that particular time that no matter what else you do or where you go, you're a Raider. If I said I wasn't, the guys would say it's bullshit. They know better."

Upshaw, who looks more like a chief executive officer of a Fortune 100 company than a former offensive lineman, is talking in his office, which is the size of a small gym.

He's sitting behind a massive, well-varnished desk surrounded by bookshelves holding not only law books and court documents, but also the NFL football register and mementos of his 16-year career with the Raiders. Adorning his office walls are well-framed prints of his Raider days and of the NFL's 75th-anniversary all-time team, of which Upshaw was selected as a guard.

His career was remarkable, considering that he was a walk-on at Texas A & I University who preferred baseball to football.

In his 16-year career from 1967 to 1981, Upshaw played in 217 games, a Raiders record, and started in 207 consecutive league games. He was a six-time Pro Bowl player, and he was offensive captain for the Raiders for nine years. He played in 24 post-season games, including three Super Bowls in three separate decades, and was elected to the Hall of Fame in his first year of eligibility in 1987.

All this from a player who played college football only after Texas A & I coach Gil Steinke spotted him killing time during freshman orientation by watching football practice and demanded that he go get a uniform and show up for the afternoon practice.

"I never did like football, and I was on the B-team until my senior year in high school, only because as a senior you had to be on the varsity," Upshaw said. "During A & I's freshman orientation, I walked over to the football field to watch and Steinke told me to get a uniform, and that's what I did. After a few days I got a partial scholarship, and after the first year, I got a full scholarship. But if I didn't go watch that practice, I wouldn't be sitting here today."

Instead, he'd probably be teaching high school somewhere, because there weren't too many options for young black men growing up in Robstown, Texas, during the late 1950s.

Upshaw was born on August 15, 1945, and growing up, segregation was very much alive in small-town south Texas.

Until high school, he went to a four-room school with eight other students in his class, and outside of class, he was either picking cotton or playing baseball.

"I attended first grade to middle school with the same eight kids," Upshaw said. "It wasn't until I got to high school that schools became desegregated."

Blacks could only go to the movies on Saturday afternoon, and they had to sit in the balcony. Everyone knew his or her place.

"Growing up, you knew you had to stay in your part of town, and the only time people were together was for Little League games, and then, after the games, everyone would disappear," Upshaw said. "You grew up with your family, your church, and baseball and that was it. But my dad never allowed us to get tangled up in prejudice. We just accepted everyone for who they were."

Eugene Upshaw Sr. was a roustabout for an oil company, and Upshaw's mother, Cora, was a domestic worker.

When Eugene got home from work, Gene and his two younger brothers had better be there.

"What was amazing was that I'd see him go to work at the same time every day and get home at the same time every day. And when he got home at 4:30, we better be there too. There was none of that wait until the next out or next inning and then come home. We had to be there."

It was baseball that the Upshaw boys played all day long, and when Gene had offers to sign out of high school, his dad, a decent pitcher in his own day, gave Gene an ultimatum.

Sign the baseball contract and never again step foot in the house, or go to college.

"What I really wanted to do was play baseball," Gene said. "But if I did, then I couldn't live at home anymore, so instead of signing, my dad gave me $75 to go register at A & I."

He walked on at Texas A & I as a 6-foot, 190-pound center, but Gil Steinke spotted potential.

Upshaw wasn't big, but he was fast for a lineman and he began to mature physically, growing five inches and gaining 50 pounds. Since he had played only one year of high school varsity football, he had to learn the game, but after four years, he was on the NFL radar.

Improbable as it would have seemed when he was a walk-on, Upshaw got invited to play in the Senior Bowl, where for the first time he matched up against better talent, giving the scouts a better gauge.

"I didn't believe I would even get drafted," he said. "I didn't think I was on that level, and then all of a sudden, I got invited to the Senior Bowl and that was the difference. I went there as a probable third-rounder and left as a legitimate first-round pick."

After the Senior Bowl, Upshaw played in the College All-Star Game and was named captain by his teammates, who a few months earlier had never heard of him.

"I didn't know anyone from Adam," he said. "I came all the way from Texas A & I to be captain of the All-Star team that included players like Bubba Smith, Alan Page, Floyd Little, and Bob Griese. Everything came together at the right time."

Upshaw raised his stock so much that the Raiders made him their first-round draft pick in 1967, the 16th pick in the league.

You'd think that given Upshaw's unheralded and improbable college football career, he would have been thrilled to be chosen by the Raiders, or any other NFL team for that matter, but he wasn't thrilled at all. In fact, he had no desire to play for Al Davis's Raiders. He wanted to play for the Atlanta Falcons, where he knew players on the team who had played at Texas A & I.

Upshaw quickly learned how the NFL worked.

"Al said he didn't give a damn what I wanted, Oakland was where I was going to play," he said. "The Raiders flew me and my parents to Oakland and we met everyone, and after that I still didn't want to play there. But it was the first year of the common draft, and I had no choice and I had no leverage."

Despite Upshaw's protestations, he signed with the Raiders and in his first year, Upshaw went from an unknown at A & I to a starting left guard for the Raiders that lost one regular-season game in 1967 and played the Green Bay Packers in the Super Bowl.

The Raiders were beaten badly by the Packers that day at Miami's Orange Bowl, but Upshaw remembers the experience more than the game.

"At halftime they had those big blow-up dolls of Packers and Raiders guys," Upshaw said. "And after the game, I went into the Packers' locker room and Ray Nitschke told me I played good and that we'd be back there a lot. That was validation, and from then on I knew we'd be back."

It took Upshaw and the Raiders nine years to get to another Super Bowl, but in Upshaw's mind, they should have gotten there every year.

"When we went to training camp, Madden would always say that we can go to the Super Bowl," Upshaw said. "There were other teams that can't go, but we can."

In between Super Bowl appearances, Upshaw's level of play grew, pushed by the arrival of Art Shell, his alter ego on the field.

"When Art showed up in my second year, I got a buddy," Upshaw said. "There was another black guy playing on the offensive line and he could . . . though he didn't start right away, you knew he could play."

The two grew close on and off the field, complementing each other with different styles.

"I didn't want to let him down and he didn't want to let me down," Upshaw said. "I was more vocal, and Art would get upset when guys would talk in the huddle. But I had the reputation for talking outside the huddle, so I got a lot of criticism, but I never talked in the huddle. I was too busy trying to see what the defense was doing."

Since Upshaw was the offensive captain, he negotiated both his and Shell's contract with Davis. Whatever Upshaw got, that's what Shell got.

"Back then it wasn't about the money," Upshaw said. "I was treated okay by the Raiders and we were winning. We didn't have the gripes most teams had. In those days, everyone wanted to be a Raider."

Davis looked to Upshaw, a veteran player, to provide leadership.

Upshaw invested heavily in the Raiders program and began to flourish, gaining respect around the team and the league. During Upshaw's third year, Davis pulled him aside and told him that he needed to step up his presence on the team. Often, Davis would consult Upshaw and a few other key veterans when he was considering bringing in a new player. Rarely would a new player be acquired without Upshaw's having a say in the matter.

"After my third year, Al called me into his office and told me I had to take more of a leadership role, and after that I was elected captain," Upshaw said. "You win as many games inside the locker room as you do on the field, and you had to buy into the program.

"Al never once got a guy in those days without talking to us and letting us know what he was thinking," Upshaw said. "That's just the way we did it. From Al on down to the guy who sweeps up when we leave, everyone knew their role in the organization. That's because Al was always around. He either had something to say to you or not, but for 16 goddamn years he'd be standing by the door and you couldn't get out without seeing him."

Off the field, Upshaw began to take a more active role in union activities, becoming more vocal about players' rights. Despite

Upshaw's involvement, Davis let him be, never allowing union issues to interfere with Upshaw's play.

Part of the reason was that Davis was a maverick himself, taking on the league in his own right. Another part was that Upshaw was making All-Pro every year and, together with Shell, was among the best linemen in football.

"There was a plantation mentality in the NFL, and out of that grew the 1970 conflict, so I was affected right away. As soon as I came into the league, there was the common draft and I was screwed out of leverage. I played where they told me to play or I didn't play at all. In my mind-set, I knew that you should be able to make choices about your life and your career and I felt like I had to speak up. In those days, if you stepped out of line, they got rid of you, but I had Davis, who knew what it was like to go against the grain. Each step of the way, Al never once got in the way."

Davis could afford to leave things be.

While other owners sent players packing after the 1970 players' strike that ended in disaster for the players when they called off the strike after a month of frustration, the Raiders stayed intact.

Though the strike caused bad blood between activist-minded players like Upshaw and veterans who didn't want to risk their careers for the good of the union, feelings were put aside when it came time to play.

"Training camp used to be hard," Upshaw said. "You had to practice hard, but then you had to run hard at night and you had to show up, too. We had guys who went to the Bamboo Room right after practice, and you had to do it. People talk about camaraderie, but it was real with us. We had guys on the team who came from the South, that grew up during segregation, and we had good old boys. I knew that I couldn't play at Alabama and that I couldn't play in the Southwest Conference, and now we were all together and out drinking with each other and you never thought about any of that stuff.

"We did things as a team. When we got together at Al's Cactus Room, you better have a goddamn good excuse if you didn't show up. When you got one of us, you got all of us, and the winning got easy because of that. When we'd show up each year in Santa Rosa, it wasn't about you liking me and inviting me to come to your house. But when we got into the alley, we'd fight together. That's what we had developed. When you think of the Raiders, you think of fear. It was: I don't care if you like me, I don't care if you hate me or if you respect me. But you'd better fear me. That was Al."

Apart from the team, Upshaw was beginning to get involved in more than football. He opened up a few bars in Oakland: the Patio, the Rainbow Room, and then Uppy's on the Square.

He established himself within Oakland political circles and became involved in the Democratic Party. It was a time of great social upheaval, and Oakland was at the forefront.

"During this period, we were right in the middle of Vietnam and all the shit that was going on in Berkeley with the Black Panther Party. And I knew all those guys like Huey Newton, Eldridge Cleaver, and Bobby Seale. They came into my bar and we'd talk. The Panthers never put any pressure on us. But politically, I could see there were things I wanted to do. I was trying to branch out from being just a football player. I was being encouraged to get involved."

But Upshaw didn't forget where his checks were coming from.

From 1972 through 1977, Upshaw made the All-Pro team and never missed a game as the Raiders dominated the AFC West, though managing one Super Bowl appearance.

"I'm still not ready to say the Steelers and the Dolphins were better teams," Upshaw said. "We were always just one play away. We should have gone to nine Super Bowls."

As his career progressed through the late 1970s, it seemed that Upshaw would never miss a game, but when he entered his third decade with the Raiders, his decline began.

His last year as an All-Pro was in 1977, but he, along with Shell, still dominated the left side of the Raiders' line.

In 1982, Upshaw arrived at a personal and professional crossroads.

It was to be his last year as a Raider. While his playing career was ending, his union duties were increasing. By that time, he was president of the NFL players' union, heavily involved in the negotiations with then-NFLPA executive director Ed Garvey, who was

Union leader Gene Upshaw

trying to hammer out a new agreement with the owners to avert a players' strike. Upshaw was being criticized by some for playing the heavy during union negotiations.

His personal life was also in turmoil. His first marriage had broken up and his father, a double amputee, was in ill health.

But in early 1983, he sat down with Davis for six hours, talking about his future, asking for advice about whether to take over for Garvey as head of the union.

"I wanted Al's opinion and we sat and talked about everything," Upshaw said. "It made my decision a lot easier."

Not long after the meeting, Upshaw took over for Garvey and moved to Washington. In June 1983, the union was under his leadership, and it became a battleground as he waged a war to win free agency.

An ugly strike in 1987 that saw owners hire replacement players brought a wave of criticism toward Upshaw, but the union prevailed. Finally, in 1993, players won the right for free agency.

Today, with labor peace well in hand, Upshaw's job is to look out for the nearly 2,000 active as well as the thousands of retired players.

"I hear from guys all over, and some of them don't know what to do or where to go," he said. "They don't call until they are over their heads, and I wonder about a lot of guys. Being a Raider gets you in the door, but it doesn't keep you there."

Eugene Upshaw

Born August 15, 1945, at Robstown, TX
Height: 6'5" Weight: 255
High School: Robstown, TX.
Received degree in secondary education from Texas A & I College. Did graduate work at California State University at Hayward.

Brother of Marvin Upshaw, defensive end with Cleveland Browns, Kansas City Chiefs, and St. Louis Cardinals, 1968 through 1976; cousin of Willie Upshaw, former first baseman–outfielder with Toronto Blue Jays.
Named to *The Sporting News* AFL All-Star Team, 1967 through 1969.
Named to *The Sporting News* AFC All-Star Team, 1970, 1971, and 1977.
Selected by Oakland AFL in 1st round (17th player selected) of 1967 AFL-NFL draft.
Oakland AFL, 1967 through 1969; Oakland NFL, 1970 through 1981.
Games: 1967 (14), 1968 (14), 1969 (14), 1970 (14), 1971 (14), 1972 (14), 1973 (14), 1974 (14), 1975 (14), 1976 (14), 1977 (14), 1978 (16), 1979 (16), 1980 (16), 1981 (15). Total AFL—42. Total NFL—185. Total Pro—217.

Pro statistics: Fumbled once, 1969 and 1970; recovered one fumble, 1979 and 1980.
　　Played in AFL All-Star Game following 1968 season.
　　Played in Pro Bowl following 1972 through 1977 seasons.
　　Played in AFL Championship Game, 1967 through 1969.
　　Played in AFC Championship Game following 1970, 1973 through 1977, and 1980 seasons.
　　Played in AFL-NFL Championship Game following 1967 season.
　　Played in NFL Championship Game following 1967, 1976, and 1980 seasons.

CLIFF BRANCH hauls in another bomb.

17

THE MONEY MAN

Cliff Branch

There are two things about Cliff Branch that should be made perfectly clear. One is that he prefers to be called Clifford, his given name, not Cliff, which is what everybody but his close friends and family call him. Cliff is just a football name—or a stage name—and he never liked it all that much.

"I prefer Clifford," he said.

The second thing that defines Cliff Branch is that he has a natural tendency to enjoy wherever he is, which at the moment is inside a dingy Kmart store located in a faceless Las Vegas neighborhood not far from the city's Juvenile Detention Center, better known to the locals as "the Juvie."

It is here, in this faded Kmart, where Branch for the next two days will sit behind a small rickety desk adorned with a dirty white vinyl sign with black lettering that reads:

Cliff Branch #21
World Champion Los Angeles Raiders

Piled on top of the desk are Branch's tools of trade: posters, trading cards, and photos (color and black-and-white) that he will sign upon request for $20, $15, and $10, respectively.

He's got the gig down pat, though he's about half an hour late from the 11 A.M. scheduled appearance that is supposed to run until 5 P.M.

After a half hour in the Kmart, it's become clear that Branch is either gregarious or patient enough not to mind having strangers come up to him and ask the same inane questions again and again.

Signing autographs inside Kmart stores is his job and, despite how depressing it may seem, it's apparently fulfilling for Branch. It is how he makes money.

"Don't I know you?" the people say, or "Didn't you used to be somebody?"

Branch will patiently answer the questions with a smile and will even give away a signed black-and-white photo to kids, but he won't personalize it. That he must charge for, because this, after all, is his livelihood.

Nevertheless, he honestly seems to enjoy the whole thing. Either that or he's a great actor, because the whole thing reeks of another depressing example of a former athlete hanging on to his past—that is, until he meets and greets the people who wander up to his table.

When people approach, he immediately disarms the visitors with a quick smile and a friendly greeting. He's especially warm to little kids, who weren't even born when he caught his last pass for the Raiders in 1985.

He's been spending his weekends at department stores around the West Coast since he retired, driving from city to city, lugging a black case filled with the posters and photos and a bunch of felt-tipped pens wrapped with a thick rubber band.

It's a low-frills enterprise, but this particular Las Vegas trip was especially enjoyable for Branch, who drove in from his home in Santa Rosa, California, with his girlfriend to spend the weekend days at the Kmart while hitting the strip at night. Branch's parents even joined in on the fun, meeting him for the weekend and taking in a Gladys Knight show at one of the strip's megahotels.

Though Branch's nearly an hour tardy, the only indication that he stayed out late the night before is a quick application of Visine to soothe his tired eyes. Once that's completed, he's ready.

Though it's been some 15 years since he last wore a Raiders uniform, there's a faint buzz in the store as people learn that some sort of celebrity is in their midst. And from the looks of it, these people haven't seen many celebrities, regardless of the fact that they live in a town that caters to the rich, famous or otherwise. For these Saturday-morning shoppers, spending a moment talking to

Cliff Branch on the job at another autograph signing

Branch, the former All-Pro receiver, seems about as close to meeting someone famous as they will ever get.

Branch relishes the attention. He chides the children for not being polite enough, "yes maam"s the older women, and gently steers potential customers toward the pricey end of the table. Yet plenty of shoppers stroll right by his table, completely unaware of or uninterested in the man behind the sign.

But even those who do recognize Branch's name don't all recognize him as a former NFL player, because he hardly looks like one.

Branch is short. The Raiders listed him at 5 feet 10, but that seems generous. Still tightly muscled for a man past his 50th birthday, he appears to be just a few pounds over his playing weight.

Wearing a pair of black jeans, running shoes, and a T-shirt, Branch looks pretty much like a typical shopper looking for a power tool, gardening supplies, or other wares at a Kmart on a Saturday morning. Despite his lack of football size, however, there is an unmistakable quality about him that suggests to people his athleticism.

It was that raw speed that got Branch noticed coming out of Houston's E. E. Worthing High School. Though he played high school football, track was where he excelled—sprinting came naturally for him, and catching the ball didn't. He was the first Texas high school athlete to ever beat a 10-second 100-yard dash. Even so, that wasn't enough to scare off scores of college recruiters.

Branch was an example of the classic "There is no substitute for speed" cliché you hear football announcers say every Sunday, so securing a college scholarship was easy for him. Staying in a program wasn't.

After high school, he first went to the University of California–Berkeley, but fled after a week.

"I had never been out of Texas," he said. "I decided to go back home."

Once back in Texas, Branch enrolled at the University of Houston and spent another week there until he decided that it wasn't for him. Finally, he went to Wharton Junior College in Texas, where he became an All-American junior college player and again attracted the interest of major college football programs.

This time, he was more prepared for college life away from home, and he accepted a scholarship to the University of Colorado, a perfect fit for his wide-open lifestyle both on and off the field.

"It was a very beautiful school and a liberated state, and I could run track and play football," Branch said.

After three years, his eligibility ran out, but by then he was known as a speed-burning punt and kickoff returner. Though he didn't graduate, he left Colorado in 1972 with two options: accept Al Davis's offer to play for the Raiders as a fourth-round draft pick, or run in the Olympic Trials, with the almost certain likelihood of making the Olympic team.

Davis and the Raiders won out handily.

"I signed my contract for a $13,000 bonus with $18,500 in my first year, $21,500 in the second, and $23,500 in third year. That was a lot of money, huh?" Branch said, laughing at the paltry salary paid him by the first contract he signed, in the spring of 1972.

Despite the salary, Branch never questioned his decision. Money talked, and this was long before any U.S. Olympic members saw any cash.

"I had just ran a 10-flat 100 in the NCAA championship and I could have gone to the Olympics, but there was no conflict at all," he said. "The Raiders were a terrific passing team. It was my dream to play professional football, and the Raiders were the kind of team that threw the football."

When draft day came in 1972, Branch waited for the phone to ring, but it never did. Instead, he heard from a friend who had heard on the radio that he was the Raiders' fourth-round pick along with linebacker Dave Dalby.

Branch was as surprised as anyone.

"I never had any contact with the Raiders whatsoever," he said. "I wasn't known for having great hands. I was a speed guy who returned kicks and punts. During the draft I remember sitting by the phone and nobody ever called me. My only contact with the Raiders was when they came out to meet me and work me out."

After his first minicamp in the spring of 1972, Branch felt the way he had following his first experiences in college, and he wanted out. Only, Al Davis wouldn't let him go.

"When I first had my minicamp I had just pulled my hamstrings and I was frustrated," Branch said. "I wanted to go home, but Al told me, 'You're our property now.'"

When training camp rolled around in July, Branch's hamstrings had healed. This time, he surprised even himself with his performance.

"When summer camp came, it was great," he said. "The Raiders knew me right off the bat and welcomed me with open arms, and I made quick adjustments. We threw the ball at Colorado, and the Raiders' system was like Colorado's, so I had a great camp. Believe it or not, I dropped a few balls in college, but in camp I did well. I beat out that year's number-one pick, Mike Siani, and the Raiders released Warren Wells."

Branch impressed the coaches so much that he was named a starter, which lasted until he dropped the first pass thrown to him in the Raiders' opener against the Steelers.

"Stabler started that day and I had a miserable performance," Branch said. "Things weren't going right and John Madden said, 'Let's go with Blanda.' So Blanda comes in and I let a pass go right through my arms. Madden then yanked me, pulled Blanda, and put in Daryle Lamonica, who threw two balls to Mike Siani. I sat on the bench for three years."

The Raiders lost that day against the Steelers, then went on to a 10–3–1 season, losing again to the Steelers in the playoffs. But Branch could barely share in the team's success. He caught a grand total of three passes that year for 41 yards and hardly impressed anyone on his kick returns. Of the 12 punts Branch returned that year, he gained 21 yards. He also ran back nine kickoffs for 191 yards.

"I was very frustrated," he said. "I was running back kickoffs and wasn't doing well there either. But in 1973, the Raiders started using a three-wide receiver offense, and I got a chance to play. Then, in 1974, Siani got hurt and they put me back in, and I made All-Pro."

It turned out to be Branch's career year: he caught 60 passes for 1,092 yards and 13 touchdowns. Branch benefited from not only his blazing speed but also from having single coverage as defenses threw double coverage at Fred Biletnikoff. Playing on the left side of the offensive line also had its benefits with left-handed Ken Stabler at quarterback.

"I got the ball a lot because I was on the left side, so Snake saw me a lot," Branch said. "Freddie caught all the double teams and I was always man-to-man."

The money play for Branch was "89 X up," and Stabler called it often beginning in 1974. Branch was always open, at least in his own mind, and he wasn't shy about telling Stabler or anyone else in the huddle.

"I was always telling Snake I could beat my guy deep, but I was so confident because I had to go against Willie Brown in practice. I worked against Willie five days a week, and it made it real easy for me come Sunday. But Kenny had total command, and we were his pawns as he pushed all the right buttons. He was captain of the ship."

Though Branch emerged as a leading receiver in 1974, he didn't really make his mark until the AFC championship game that year against the Pittsburgh Steelers, when he had nine catches for 190 yards. It was a performance that got Steelers All-Pro defensive back Mel Blount benched.

"Blount couldn't stop me," Branch said. "So Chuck Noll benched him. But the next year when we played them again in the playoffs, I didn't have one catch."

The 1974 season proved to be pivotal for Branch in other areas.

After that season, he began to work more closely with perennial All-Pro receiver Biletnikoff, who helped him learn the subtleties of the game and the wide receiver position.

"After 1974 I started watching Freddy," Branch said. "He was so intense. If he dropped a ball in practice, he'd 'motherfuck' the ball down the field. Whatever he did, I tried to emulate. I'd tape my arms and use stickum, which wasn't legal, but if that's what it took, then we did it. Freddie would come in at halftime and smoke cigarettes, but I didn't get that intense, though my focus was there. We became good friends and we'd watch game film and do a lot of things socially together. Whenever I'd see him I'd always call him daddy, and he'd always answer, 'Hello, son.' I owe a lot to him."

Around this time, things began to turn for Branch off the field, as well. His success had brought fame, and fame brought some trouble.

"I was married and was happy, but then things changed," he said. "I made All-Pro and started chasing girls, and that caused problems at home. I ended up getting divorced."

But Branch's marriage problems did little to affect his play.

He made All-Pro from 1974 through 1977. The Raiders played in five consecutive AFC championship games from 1973 to 1977.

Inside the Raiders, Branch became the self-styled "Money Man." He became known for always coaxing a little extra cash out of head coach John Madden.

"John treated me great," Branch said. "I'd sit by him in the film room, and he'd say that if I got a couple of catches, he'd slip me a $100 here and there, and that's why I was the Money Man."

The Raiders' reputation as a wide-open organization that cared only about what happened on Sundays sat well with Branch, whose marriage to a white woman would not have been well received by other NFL teams during the early 1970s.

"We were very liberal and guys partied, but that never stopped us from getting the job done," Branch said. "There was just this closeness. Al had no prejudices, and we were able to pick up players who had problems with other teams, and Al would bring them in and they'd have no problems. If you wanted to be a hippie or a Hell's Angel, that was fine as long as you played Raiders football. John gave us plenty of rope, and breaking curfew was encouraged. He knew guys were going to do it anyway, and we had some guys who could hang out. Snake could be out all night and then throw three touchdown passes. Ted Hendricks showed up with a horse and rode around the practice field. It was amazing."

After the Raiders beat the Vikings in Super Bowl XI, the Raiders' dominance began to slip. But Branch's play remained consistent. Though he caught just 33 passes in 1977, he came back and caught 49 passes in 1978 and 59 passes in 1979 as the Raiders missed the playoffs under head coach Tom Flores, who had replaced Madden after the 1977 season.

"In 1976, we had won 14 straight including the Super Bowl, and we beat the shit out of the Vikings in the Super Bowl," Branch said. "And the following year we were back against the Denver Broncos' Orange Crush defense, but we had some injuries and lost in the AFC championship game. We were an aging team, and then John quit. I guess he was taking a lot of Maalox, but he was the kind of coach who played the game with us. I hated it when he retired. Then Freddie [Biletnikoff] quit and things got a lot tighter. Guys were getting fined and there was a curfew. Nothing against Tom [Flores], but things were just different."

Things changed a lot more for Branch and the Raiders after the team left Oakland in 1982. Not only were some of the Raiders' core players gone, but so was the Oakland home-field advantage.

"Playing in Oakland was a three- to seven-point advantage, because the fans were so dedicated," Branch said. "But when we moved, we lost a lot of the closeness and camaraderie. Los Angeles is such a big town and players lived all over. Guys would get out of practice and wanted to get home. We lost a lot of the mystique."

After the Raiders moved to Los Angeles, Branch's production began to drop.

In 1982, the team's first year in L.A., he caught 41 passes, and though he caught 39 passes in 1984, he caught just 27 in 1985.

After 14 years with the Raiders, Branch was on his way out.

"Al told me it was time to retire, but I didn't want to give it up," he said. "I was the littlest Raider and played 14 years without a major injury. But Al was very good to me. He told me that it was time and that at some point he'd have to release me. How many owners could tell you that?"

After he left the Raiders, Branch stayed in southern California, drifting around with no plans. Two years later, he got back into football, only it wasn't anywhere near the NFL. He spent a season playing for the Los Angeles Cobras in the Arena Football League, a debased version of the NFL game that's played indoors on a 60-yard field. For the past decade, Branch has been making his living on the weekends, bouncing from Kmart to Kmart peddling his name and cashing in on the Raiders mystique of yesteryear.

"I didn't do anything for a couple of years, but I probably should have done something," he said. "I spent my money a little bit living in Downey, California, so the Cobras called me and I played for one year. I had to play both ways—so I'd catch a touchdown pass and then turn around and play defense and give up a touchdown. But it was fun."

Though Branch said he made around $650,000 in his last year with the Raiders, he believes that today's NFL players are more interested in money than they are in winning football games.

"We made our money by getting into the playoffs, so we *had* to get into the playoffs," he said. "I made All-Pro in 1974 and got $5,000 in incentives for being All-League. I went in the next year and Al said that we needed to knock that incentive in half because I was going to make All-Pro. I don't know how much desire today's players have anymore. They make so much money that they don't care."

"The Raiders always had tight ends that made All-Pro but now they don't throw the ball to the tight end anymore. We played a vertical game, and now it's the West Coast style of play. They are going east and west and we were moving north and south. It's a different game and kind of frustrating. I asked one of the [recent] Raiders about getting one of these Super Bowl rings and he said 'Shit, I can go out and buy me one of those rings. I got enough money to buy one.' That was the attitude I've heard from some of the players."

Then again, Branch never had to worry much about getting hit. His career was played on the fringes of the field, away from the head-hunting linebackers and safeties.

"I was always begging to go deep," he said. "I never had to go across the middle a lot, because I was The Money Man and you don't mess with the money."

Clifford (Cliff) Branch

Born August 1, 1948, at Houston, TX
Height: 5'11" Weight: 170
High School: Houston, TX, E. E. Worthing.
Attended Wharton County Junior College and University of Colorado.

Tied NFL record for longest completed passing play from scrimmage when he caught a 99-yard touchdown pass from quarterback Jim Plunkett against Washington Redskins, October 2, 1983.
Named as wide receiver on *The Sporting News* AFC All-Star Team, 1974 and 1976.
Selected by Oakland in 4th round (98th player selected) of 1972 NFL draft.
Franchise transferred to Los Angeles, May 7, 1982.
On injured reserve with hamstring injury, August 23 through October 23, 1985; activated after clearing procedural waivers, October 25, 1985.

Year	Club	G.	Att.	Yds.	Avg.	TD	P.C.	Yds.	Avg.	TD	TD	Pts.	F.
			RUSHING				**PASS RECEIVING**				**TOTAL**		
1972	Oakland NFL	14	1	5	5.0	0	3	41	13.7	0	0	0	2
1973	Oakland NFL	13			None		19	290	15.3	3	3	18	0
1974	Oakland NFL	13			None		60	*1092	18.2	*13	13	78	1
1975	Oakland NFL	14	2	18	9.0	0	51	893	17.5	9	9	54	0
1976	Oakland NFL	14	3	12	4.0	0	46	1111	24.2	*12	12	72	0
1977	Oakland NFL	13			None		33	540	16.4	6	6	36	0
1978	Oakland NFL	16			None	0	49	709	14.5	1	1	6	2
1979	Oakland NFL	14	1	4	4.0	0	59	844	14.3	6	6	36	1
1980	Oakland NFL	16	1	1	1.0	0	44	858	19.5	7	7	42	0
1981	Oakland NFL	16			None		41	635	15.5	1	1	6	0
1982	Los Angeles Raiders NFL	9	2	10	5.0	0	30	575	19.2	4	4	24	0
1983	Los Angeles Raiders NFL	12	1	20	20.0	0	39	696	17.8	5	5	30	3
1984	Los Angeles Raiders NFL	14			None		27	401	14.9	0	0	0	0
1985	Los Angeles Raiders NFL	4			None				None		0	0	0
	Pro Totals—14 Years	182	11	70	6.4	0	501	8685	17.3	67	67	402	6

Additional pro statistics: Returned 12 punts for 21 yards and nine kickoffs for 191 yards, 1972; recovered one fumble, 1974; recovered two fumbles, 1984.
Played in AFC Championship Game following 1973 through 1977, 1980 and 1983 seasons.
Played in NFL Championship Game following 1976, 1980, and 1983 seasons.
Played in Pro Bowl following 1974 through 1977 seasons.

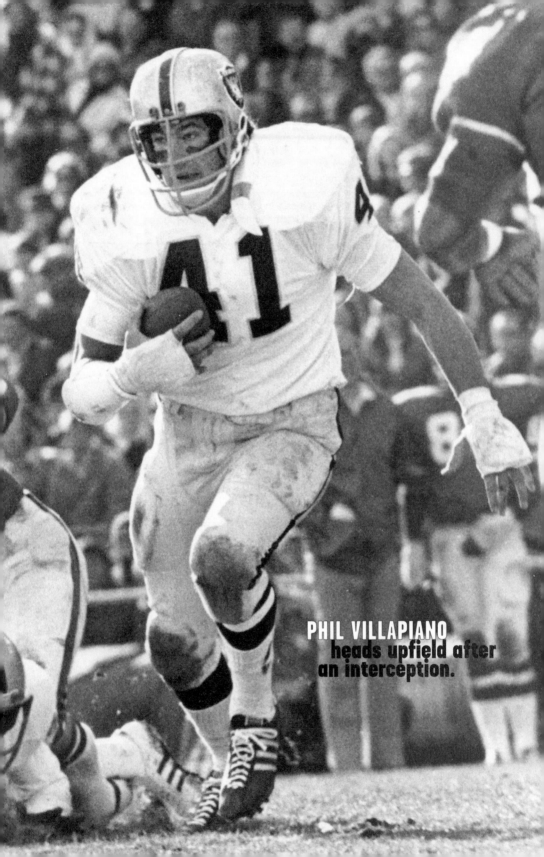

PHIL VILLAPIANO heads upfield after an interception.

18

PHIL VILLAPIANO

It's hard to envision anywhere more dreary than northern New Jersey on a gray winter day, where the landscape—all swamplands, oil refineries, and interstate—seems impossibly drab. And as if the picture outside my car needed any more ugliness, a raging warehouse fire was spewing black smoke over the highway, like some sort of twisted toxic welcome in case visitors failed to see the place for what it really is.

It is here, in Union, New Jersey, a scruffy town located some 10 miles from Newark, that Phil Villapiano works as a senior vice president of an oceangoing shipping company.

Villapiano spent nine years terrorizing quarterbacks for the Raiders, playing opposite Hall of Famer Ted Hendricks at outside linebacker, and on most Sundays, it was hard to tell who was better. Twenty years removed from the Raiders, Villapiano works out of his Union, New Jersey, office when he's not traveling across the country, selling space on those massive freighters. It's not nearly as glamorous as chasing NFL quarterbacks, but it's not as painful, either, and it provides a good enough living to allow Villapiano and his second wife, Susan, and their son to afford the country-club life. A good enough living to have some of his former teammates call from time to time and ask for help, financial or otherwise.

And Villapiano swears it's all because he played for the Raiders.

"I work like a Raider, think like a Raider, and I talk like a Raider even to this day," he said. "I even drive my car like a fucking Raider. I loved being a part of it, and it still pisses me off when they don't play well."

Though he has pictures of his Raiders days hanging on his office wall to prove his self-confessed loyalty to the team, he is truly pure Jersey, right down to his acquaintance with New Jersey's favorite son, Bruce Springsteen.

Villapiano played nearly a decade in Oakland, then two seasons in Buffalo after Al Davis shrewdly dealt the aging linebacker for star receiver Bob Chandler in 1980. While Villapiano had the silk-shirted, pink-suited California look down pat, he really never left the swamplands and faded beach towns of the Jersey Shore.

He grew up in Asbury Park, a decayed resort town that used to cater to tourists until the town was torched during the race riots in the early 1970s, driving the beach clubs out of business.

But to Villapiano, who graduated from Ocean Township High School in 1967, Asbury Park evokes idyllic memories of football games, beach parties, and drinking in bars like the Student Prince, where Villapiano used to listen to some local kid named Springsteen try to be a rock star.

And while Villapiano may still have an allegiance to Asbury Park, that doesn't mean he lives there. Instead, he makes his home in upscale Rumson, where all the Jersey kids who made good live.

"When I grew up, Asbury Park was the best city in the whole eastern seaboard," he said. "That town was a melting pot. We had everybody. I knew blacks, Puerto Ricans, Jews, Italians, and it was a wonderful place to grow up in. It is a shame what happened to that town."

Phil is the middle brother of three boys, sandwiched between his older brother Gus and younger brother John. He also has a younger sister, and all the kids except Gus went to Bowling Green (Ohio) University courtesy of athletic scholarships.

The athletic prowess surprised no one in Asbury Park, given that both of Villapiano's parents were schoolteachers and Villapiano's father also coached and was athletic director in the Asbury Park high school system.

"My dad was a pretty famous athlete around here," Phil said. "All the Italians in town came from the same place in Italy, and everyone knew each other. There were a lot of railroad people and it was very blue collar, but my dad went to college at DePauw University in Indiana and came back and coached in the school system. He had a lot to do with us being into sports. Our baby-sitter was Asbury Park football and baseball games. The cool thing was that during the football season, all the equipment was in our garage. My dad was so busy that he never saw me play until I was in high school, but both were very good parents and good teachers. They forced us to study and gave us our work ethic."

There's still a little schoolboy left in Villapiano, though he was born in 1949. He was hardwired as a player, and much of the wattage still burns. He played linebacker at 6-foot-2, 225, smallish for his position, and he lacked the compactness of build that you normally think of when you picture an NFL linebacker.

Villapiano made up for whatever physical shortcomings he had on the field with good speed and a fiery, high-strung nature that allowed him to play with reckless abandon.

Today he looks fit, and he is much lighter than his 225-pound playing weight, which eases the strain on both of his surgically repaired knees. His face is thin, framed by narrow eyes, and his hair is flecked with gray. Villapiano agreed to meet me in his office the day after returning from a business trip. He hardly looks like an executive vice president, wearing a pair of jeans with a tan button-down long-sleeved shirt and a pair of running shoes, as he fields phone calls and wades through piles of papers scattered on his desk. His voice is raspy and he talks fast while bantering on the phone. He laughs easily as he recalls the often absurd moments of being an NFL football player.

Like the time he became a favorite among the heavily Hispanic crowd in San Diego.

"It was my second game as a Raider and we were playing in San Diego, and the coaches warned me that they were going to run at me and I was so fucking fired up," he said, accentuating his story with arm gesticulations. "I made the first tackle of the game and the announcer said, 'Tackle by Veeyapiano,' like I had a Spanish last name. Well, I must have had 30 tackles that game, and the announcer kept calling my name like I was Spanish. 'Tackle by Veeyapiano, tackle by Veeyapiano'—over and over again. So after the game, I'm in the locker room and a Mexican cop comes in and tells me a group of people want to talk to me. So I walk down the hall and the cop opens the door and there are 200 Mexicans screaming, 'Veeyapiano, Veeyapiano, Veeyapiano.' I couldn't believe it. I jumped down there and drank beer with them, and I fucking loved it. They thought I was Spanish, but it was so nice of these people that I never told them my real name."

As a Raider, Villapiano was one of the team's social chairmen, organizing all kinds of games and tournaments in training camp and during the season. He organized the infamous air hockey tournaments to help break up the monotony, along with weekly golf outings, bowling games, and other extracurricular activities.

"I was absolutely born to be a Raider. There was no other team," he said. "I fit in perfectly. When I hit people, I knew I could hurt them, and off the field, I knew how to go out. I was so fucking proud to wear black and be hated. I used to get the chills when we'd go to Pittsburgh and get booed. I just couldn't wait to hit somebody hard."

The impatience to hurt opposing ballcarriers is a good quality to have on the defensive side of an NFL field, but what got Villapiano to the Raiders as much as anything else was an almost uncanny sense of timing.

Though he was a standout running back and middle linebacker in high school, he didn't draw much interest from big colleges except the University of Maryland, the only school with a major football program to offer him a scholarship. But Lou Saban, then Maryland's football coach, left the school and Villapiano backed out.

"I liked Maryland, but Saban walked, and now all that was left was all these little schools," he said. "My father knew about Bowling Green, so we drove out there. It was hardly a football factory, but it was draft day the day I visited and five Bowling Green guys got drafted. I said, 'Holy shit, you get drafted out there,' and by the end of the day, I signed up."

Villapiano was recruited to play linebacker, but on the first day of practice, he took one look at the size of the linebackers and jumped into a group of defensive ends going through drills.

"That first day there must have been a hundred freshmen trying out for the team, and I was about to get into the linebacker line, but then I went into the defensive-end line because they all looked so skinny," he said. "The funny thing was, the coaches didn't even know the difference. They had no clue who I was. I was tall and thin and I was doing great, so they left me there, but I wished I had played linebacker. It would have helped me when I got to the Raiders."

Villapiano didn't start at Bowling Green until the middle of his sophomore year, and though he was small for the defensive line, he dominated.

"I was okay in high school, but I got better in college," he said. "I could rush the passer and was confident that I could tackle anybody. But I was also very coachable, and I was really lucky."

When the pro scouts starting showing up at Bowling Green, Villapiano knew it was his chance to get noticed—and he took full advantage.

"One day, a whole bunch of scouts were at practice and my coach pulled me aside and said, 'Phil, this is a big day for you.' So I ran a 4.6 40-yard dash in full equipment, and then did it three times in a row."

It was enough to put Villapiano on the NFL's radar screen, and it won him an invitation to the Blue-Gray Game after his senior season.

Again, he knew it was an opportunity to make an impression.

"I went down there and played fucking hard and partied hard at night. But I made a ton of tackles and got invited to the Senior Bowl."

Now he was really beginning to garner the scouts' interest, but he knew that because he played at a small school, many of the scouts were still skeptical. He needed a big game in the Senior Bowl to solidify his chances of getting drafted.

"That game was the whole draft, but on the opening kickoff, I ran into an elbow that caught me right in the eye and I couldn't see because the eye was closed," he said. "But I still played with one eye and tackled everybody. After the game, Al Davis grabbed me and said, 'Nice game, son,' and I couldn't believe that it was Davis right there on the field. That really helped me."

When Villapiano returned to Bowling Green after playing in the Senior Bowl, his phone started ringing off the hook. Scouts had suddenly realized that he fit the NFL's emerging prototype of bigger, faster linebackers.

Listening to predictions that he'd be picked within the first three rounds, Villapiano decided he'd throw himself a draft party with the $2,000 he got from playing in the Senior Bowl. When the Raiders called to tell him he had been drafted in the second round, he made an immediate Raider-like impression.

"The $2,000 was more money than I saw in my whole life, so I got about 20 guys together and had this big party," he said. "Everyone was saying I'd go in the first three rounds, and the draft started around 10 in the morning, so we started drinking around 10 A.M. By four in the afternoon, I still didn't know I was drafted, so I figured things just didn't work out and we really started to drink. I got so blasted. And then the phone rings and it was Ron Wolf on the phone, and he tells me that the Raiders were happy to draft me, and I said, 'Where the fuck have you guys been all day?' Ron started cracking up and asks me if I'm all right to talk to the press, and then all the writers started calling and it was cool."

Then the serious business of being a Raider began in earnest. In his first minicamp with the team in April, Villapiano suffered a badly sprained ankle. Then he went back out to Oakland and pulled a hamstring. It was in the annual College All-Star Game that he started to impress.

"I kicked ass the night against the Colts, but then I go to Santa Rosa for training camp and I was scared to death," he said.

As a defensive end in college, Villapiano never had to cover any receivers coming out of the backfield. But the Raiders had no plans for him to play on the defensive line, instead throwing him into the starting lineup as a linebacker.

"Everyone was ahead of me, but there were some injuries, and within the first week I'm starting and I have no fucking clue," he said. "I didn't know how to cover anyone. But they needed some tacklers, and after a few preseason games, I started to do pretty good. I just didn't know what I was doing."

In those early days, Villapiano was so unfamiliar with his assignments that he had to rely on veterans such as middle linebacker Dan Connors to tell him where to play. As the offense would line up, Villapiano would frantically ask Connors for help. Connors would position Villapiano correctly, and the rookie would unleash his fury on the ballcarriers, relying on instinct and aggression to make up for his lack of knowledge.

"I was very coachable and I studied hard, but I think I took 10 years off Dan Connors's life," Villapiano said. "I never weighed more than 225 pounds, but when you're a player, you're a player. All I wanted to do was to make the kickoff team. I respected everyone and I just worked."

His first true test came in the Raiders' final preseason game, against the Colts in Jacksonville, Florida, on a steamy August night.

Though still an unsure and untested rookie, he teed off against the Colts, proving to the veterans and the Raiders coaches that he could handle himself.

"I played defense and on all the special teams, and it must have been 100 degrees," he said. "I had already had a fight with Tom Matte in the College All-Star Game, and we went at it."

Villapiano did more than just make the kickoff team. As an immediate starter, he progressed quickly and ended up surprising even himself by being named the NFL's Defensive Rookie of the Year.

"I got started by luck and the breaks fell for me, but once I got in there, I did good," he said. "I just needed to learn more. Connors was good to me, and the coaches were patient. I caught up on the field. Davis and Madden would say to me, 'fuck coverage, you got guys behind you.' It was the right time and they needed outside linebackers that could run. When I went to the Pro Bowl, there was me and guys like Ted Hendricks and Jack Ham. But Davis always brought on guys that could win."

It may have taken a while before Villapiano felt comfortable on the field, but he took to the Raiders lifestyle immediately.

The rookies and other younger players formed what they called the "junior board" to compete in off-the-field activities with the team's "senior board," made up of Raiders veterans like Ken Stabler and Pete Banaszak.

"We weren't shy, and I was out there with the best of them," Villapiano said. "I liked the ladies. I liked the travel, and I liked to party."

One of the Raiders' traditions involved Camaraderie Night, when the whole team would go out and drink, usually on Thursday nights, the idea being that the team that gets drunk together, stays together. While it may have helped ruin a few marriages, it also helped create a bond among the players that carried over to the field.

"We'd party all night, but all of the things we did off the field helped in the fourth quarter when we needed to win, because we knew each other inside and out," Villapiano said. "You had to be [at Camaraderie Night], and we were too happy to be together. We didn't want anybody like wives, kids, or anybody else interfering. We wanted to travel hard together, and laugh hard together, and show up the next morning and do it all over again."

The Raiders could also thank Villapiano for sending a Coleco air hockey game to training camp in Santa Rosa, helping to create the legendary air hockey tournament designed to break the monotony of camp and boost team morale.

"During an off-season basketball game against the Rams, they asked me at halftime to race Isiah Robertson on one of those teeny tricycle bikes, and whoever won got the air hockey table. I won and sent it up to Santa Rosa and started the tournament," he said.

The tournament brought everyone together, and with Villapiano as self-appointed commissioner, the rules were set. Everyone had to cheat and be drunk. The tournament proved to be so popular that soon the Raiders' beat writers, bored and needing good copy from training camp, wrote about the Gus Otto Memorial Tournament, named after the recently retired Raiders linebacker.

"There was a spread in the *San Francisco Chronicle* and the press was getting involved, so I called to thank the Coleco people," Villapiano said. "They called back and asked if we wanted to have an awards dinner. I got everyone to show up for a Coleco/Raiders awards dinner with the Coleco people on one side of the room and the Raiders on the other, with a head table and everything. When they brought the food out, I don't know who threw the first roll, but pretty soon there was this huge fucking food fight with prime ribs flying across the room. It was unbelievable. Don Shinnick, our linebackers coach, came up to get his award, crawled under the head table, and stuck his hand up. As his hand came up from under the table, people were throwing buns and shit at his hand. This went on all night."

The food fight wouldn't have attracted much attention, except that the local media were at the dinner and the antics were all captured on film, making for a compelling newscast that night.

The only guy who seemed to care was crusty veteran George Blanda.

"The next morning at practice, Blanda came up to me and said, 'You and your fucking friends are a disgrace to the Oakland Raiders. Who do you think you are, acting like fucking babies, you fucking assholes.' We let it go," Villapiano said.

Villapiano was much more serious on the field. He was a vicious player who not only wanted to make a tackle but wanted to inflict some pain as well.

"We liked our image and liked the way people thought of us," he said. "Guys like Jack Tatum and George Atkinson would hurt you, and I was one of them. When I hit people, I knew I could hurt them. There were times when I grabbed an opposing player and told him to get back to the huddle because they had no idea that they were about to get hurt."

Villapiano was named Defensive Rookie of the Year in 1971, but he didn't make All-Pro until the 1973 season. Then he strung together five consecutive Pro Bowl seasons and capped off the 1976 season by making All-Pro as the Raiders beat the Vikings 32–14 to win the Super Bowl.

The score wasn't close, but it was Villapiano who changed the complexion of the game early in the first half by forcing a fumble after the Vikings blocked a Ray Guy punt, recovering the ball on the Raiders' three-yard line.

"On first down, they sweep us and we get them down," Villapiano said. "On second down, they lined up in their 'Jumbo' offense, and we had practiced against it so I knew they only had two plays. They are lining up, and I'm screaming, 'We got them right where we want them.' Ron Yary was opposite me, and I beat the fucker and the ball popped loose."

The following year, 1977, Villapiano's body began to break down. He tore ligaments in his knee against the Steelers in the second game of the season, forcing him to miss the rest of the year.

When he came back in 1978, the Raiders made him the weakside linebacker.

"I had an attitude about it. I wanted things the way they used to be," he said.

The game was changing, too, with defenses becoming more situational, causing the coaches to substitute for players like Villapiano.

"I didn't like all that substitution shit," he said. "I couldn't even get a sweat going."

The coaches switched Villapiano to middle linebacker in 1979, but Al Davis decided he was an aging but still valuable commodity, so he traded him to the Buffalo Bills for All-Pro receiver Bob Chandler.

It was the last thing Villapiano expected to hear when Al Davis called him in May 1980.

"I was home in New Jersey and just got back from church, and the phone rings and it's Al," Villapiano said. "We used to talk football a lot, and he asked me what I thought about Bob Chandler, and I said he could fucking play. Freddie [Biletnikoff] had retired and Cliff [Branch] had a bad year, and things weren't going so good. So he said, 'Do you think Chandler can be an Oakland Raider?' I asked what he had to give up to get him, and he said, 'you.'" I kinda laughed, and I said, 'Am I gone?,' and Al said, 'You're gone.'"

Villapiano balked at going east, but his father-in-law from his first marriage told him to shut up, make the money, and help the team.

"I was pissed off, but he said, 'Phil, don't you understand. You've had your day, so now go and make the fucking money,' so I went and played for four years. I became a great cheerleader and made more money my last four years than I did up until then," he said.

Before leaving Oakland, Villapiano fortuitously called on an aquaintance he had made a few years earlier who was starting his own shipping business and had asked Villapiano to join the company. But that was when Villapiano wanted no part of anything that wasn't football, and he declined.

"He said, 'When you grow up, call me,' and after I hurt my knee, I called him up and spent five off-seasons working with the company," Villapiano said.

When Villapiano blew out his other knee in 1983, he retired and went to work with the shipping company, but the transition out of the NFL proved devastating.

"In October 1983, I blew my knee out," he said. "In February 1984, my dad died. In April, I started my new career, and in May, my wife and I said our marriage was over after nine years. I was the worst husband in the world, but our marriage didn't suck, we just got done with football."

Villapiano got divorced and began weaning himself off his 13 years in the NFL.

"Now, all of a sudden, I'm coming home from work beat up from a new career and you're a rookie again. I went from making around $200,000 to $40,000, and that hurts. But I started to fight back. Luckily, I did something in the off-season. For some reason, some guys have a crazy thing that maybe they won't be football players anymore if they take up another occupation. But you're always a football player and you always did a great thing. It is just over."

After helping build up the shipping company, Villapiano remarried and had a son. Just after the baby was born, his wife was diagnosed with breast cancer and underwent bone-marrow transplants.

"Then we got a real problem," Villapiano said. "We have an infant and my wife has a bone-marrow transplant, but we started fighting another battle. It was a good test to see what you're made of."

Maybe it's because of his life after his Raiders days, or maybe it's just a long time gone from the NFL, but Villapiano can't understand why other players haven't been able to move away from the game they played so long ago.

"It really bothers me to see some of my friends who have not progressed beyond signing autographs," he said. "For some reason, a lot of people can't let it die. I've had guys call me begging for jobs, and I bust my ass to set them up and then they don't want to work. But you've got to lower yourself out of the big bullshit and into a normal life."

Philip (Phil) James Villapiano

Born February 26, 1949, at Long Branch, NJ
Height: 6'2" Weight: 225
High Schools: Asbury Park, NJ, and Oakhurst, NJ, Ocean Township.
Received bachelor of science degree in physical education
from Bowling Green State University in 1971.

Brother of John Villapiano, linebacker with Houston-Shreveport franchise in WFL, 1974.
Named to *The Sporting News* AFC All-Star Team, 1974.
Selected by Oakland in 2nd round (45th player selected) of 1971 NFL draft.
On injured reserve with knee injury, September 27 through remainder of 1977 season.
Traded by Oakland Raiders to Buffalo Bills for wide receiver Bob Chandler, April 22, 1980.
On injured reserve with knee injury, September 28 through remainder of 1983 season.

Year	Club	INTERCEPTIONS				
		G.	No.	Yds.	Avg.	TD
1971	Oakland NFL	14	2	25	12.5	0
1972	Oakland NFL	14	3	97	32.3	1
1973	Oakland NFL	14	1	6	6.0	0
1974	Oakland NFL	14			None	
1975	Oakland NFL	14	3	32	16.0	0
1976	Oakland NFL	14	1	0	0.0	0
1977	Oakland NFL	2			None	
1978	Oakland NFL	16	2	0	0.0	0
1979	Oakland NFL	16			None	
1980	Buffalo NFL	16			None	
1981	Buffalo NFL	16			None	
1982	Buffalo NFL	9			None	
1983	Buffalo NFL	4			None	
	Pro Totals—13 Years	163	11	160	14.5	1

Additional pro statistics: Recovered two fumbles, 1971, 1972, 1975, and 1978; recovered three fumbles, 1973; recovered one fumble for 27 yards, 1974; recovered one fumble, 1976 and 1981; credited with one safety, 1978; recovered four fumbles, 1979.

Played in AFC Championship Game following 1973 through 1976 seasons.
Played in NFL Championship Game following 1976 season.
Played in Pro Bowl following 1973 through 1975 seasons.

FRED BILETNIKOFF hauls in another touchdown pass. Note the stickum on his socks.

19

FRED BILETNIKOFF

In his 14-year Raiders career, Fred Biletnikoff was a master at running pass patterns so precise that defensive backs—the most athletic players on the field—couldn't quite cover the Hall of Fame receiver.

It wasn't as if Biletnikoff was hard to catch—he was hardly a world-class sprinter—it was that his obsession with running correct routes enabled him to stay just a half-step ahead of the defense, frustrating the cornerbacks as they gave chase to someone seemingly so slow-footed. The effect was that he seemed to be always open, always able to find that small, available patch of grass along the sideline or in the corner of an end zone.

Biletnikoff displayed that same elusive quality when it came to talking to me about his career.

This is how the typical conversation would go between me and him: I'd call him up and ask for some time to talk. He'd agreeably set a time for us to talk. Then I'd call to confirm, and he, nicely enough, would tell me to call back in an hour. I'd dutifully call back in an hour, and he would tell me how busy he was and then tell me to call back in another hour. This would go on maddeningly for as long as I allowed myself to participate in the exercise in futility.

Until one day when Biletnikoff decided he'd talk. And to his credit, it was just weeks before the NFL draft, when he, as an assistant coach for the Raiders, was unusually busy helping the Raiders determine who was worthy of the millions of dollars the team would soon spend on a thoroughly examined group of 21-year-old kids.

But first a few facts on the Hall of Fame receiver who was as durable as he was surehanded.

Biletnikoff played for the Raiders from 1965 through 1978, and during his career, the Raiders never had a losing season. In a total of 190 regular-season games, he caught 589 passes for 8,974 yards and 76 touchdowns. He was the Most Valuable Player in the Raiders' 1977 Super Bowl win over the Minnesota Vikings. He caught a total of 70 passes for 1,167 yards and scored 10 touchdowns in postseason play, second in NFL history. After retiring in 1979, he was voted into the NFL's Hall of Fame in 1988.

While Biletnikoff's routine display of one-handed catches and delicate footwork looked effortless, none of it came easily. At 6 feet 1 and 190 pounds, he was not a silky smooth type of receiver. He was not flashy, like Clifford Branch, the speed-burning wide-out who played opposite Biletnikoff, nor was he overpowering. But he was exact, precise, and studious, qualities that helped put him in the Hall of Fame.

To Biletnikoff, the glamour of being a professional football player meant little. What really mattered seemed simple yet was so difficult to execute during the mayhem of a football game: running the proper route and then catching the ball. And he drove himself to perfect his craft, staying on the field after practice, running endless patterns until he could do it right not just once, but over and over again. Then he'd hit a speed bag to improve his hand-eye coordination, a trick he learned from his father, who was a national AAU boxing champion fighting out of his hometown of Erie, Pennsylvania.

The effort brought Biletnikoff a strong instinct for the game. He never really needed to see where he was on the field. Instead, he could sense it, his keen awareness honed by his perfectionist approach.

He'd argue fiercely with anyone who challenged his approach, questioned his comprehension of the game, or criticized in ignorance. Quarterbacks, coaches, even owner Al Davis would draw a profane and heated response from Biletnikoff over various slights.

"As a player, there is a lot of intensity, so when our year would start, my relationship with Al was all business," he said. "Other than that, my relationship with him has been good."

Whereas the Raiders' other receivers exhibited pure speed and other natural abilities, Biletnikoff was one part technician on the field, a surgeon carving the right path to get open to catch the ball, and one part pure will, the desire to succeed propelled by an intensity that bordered on obsessive.

"I was just really critical about myself," he said. "It was practice and games, and everything else was secondary. I was consumed by the game. I had my good times off the field, but I always felt that if I'm on the team and supposed to be contributing then I had to make sure that I was successful. I never wanted to be the one to make a mistake."

On top of the will to win, Biletnikoff was as superstitious and ritualistic toward the game as a voodoo doctor.

Nothing illustrated his obsession in catching the football as much as a substance called stickum. He slathered the yellowish glue all over his hands; it was supposed to help the ball stick. He was so enamored with the product that he'd put globs of the stuff on the inside of his socks or on the inside of his taped forearms to keep a supply at the ready. By the end of a game, the goopy substance was all over his jersey and all over the game balls. The NFL eventually banned stickum.

"But I never used it in practice," Biletnikoff said. "It was more like a psychological thing for me. It was something that made me feel comfortable on Sunday."

Biletnikoff took a similar approach to his uniform. He wore a set of old, floppy shoulder pads that looked like they were straight out of a junior varsity locker room. Yet he wouldn't dare think to have the equipment manager get him a new set for fear of disturbing the delicate football karma.

And those flimsy old shoulder pads were about the only thing protecting him other than his helmet. Toward the end of his career, he shunned wearing thigh and knee pads for fear of having the equipment slow him down. Besides, he wasn't going to run anyone over when he caught the ball, so why not take the advantage of running a bit lighter than a fully armored defensive back?

On top of Biletnikoff's talents and desire was a studious

approach to the game. He would spend hours studying game films, looking for tendencies in other teams' defenses to give him an edge. He'd adjust his routes, break off patterns—anything to find a seam in the defense. When there was a key down to be made, more often than not quarterback Ken Stabler would look first to Biletnikoff

"Statistics weren't that important to me," Biletnikoff said. "What really mattered was understanding the situations we were in and what I had to do in that particular situation."

It was a blue-collar style that fit in well with his blue-collar background.

Born on February 23, 1943, Biletnikoff grew up in Erie, Pennsylvania, in an athletic family. Not only was his father an AAU boxing champion, but his younger brother, Bob, was an outfielder in the New York Yankees organization.

At Technical Memorial High School in Erie, Biletnikoff was a star athlete, lettering in football, basketball, baseball, and track, but it was at Florida State University where he developed into a superstar receiver, setting school records for catches as an All-American receiver.

He topped off his college career against highly ranked Oklahoma in the 1965 Gator Bowl, where he caught 13 passes for 192 yards and four touchdown receptions.

His college career was so dominating that the nation's top college receiver every year is given the Biletnikoff Award.

Though Biletnikoff set virtually all of Florida State's receiving awards, he wasn't a first-round draft pick. Instead, he was drafted in the second round of the 1965 draft by both the Raiders and the Detroit Lions—this was in the days when the AFL and the NFL held separate drafts.

But he gave little thought to joining the well-established NFL. He knew that the Raiders' vertical offense was a much better fit for him, so he took his chances on the still-wildcat AFL.

"I didn't want to go back east to Detroit," he said. "There were better opportunities in playing in Oakland. I was really more interested in the Raiders because of the passing-style offense. It was the beginning of the new league, and I felt my chances were better."

Biletnikoff's instincts were correct, though he wouldn't know it for a couple of years.

While he was one of the nation's leading collegiate receivers, he was unprepared for the professional game. His first year he caught just 24 passes for no touchdowns, and in his second year, a knee injury limited him to just 17 passes for three touchdowns. Not even Biletnikoff himself had any idea that he would develop into such a prolific receiver.

"I wasn't able to handle the transition from college to the Raiders," he said. "It was very competitive and more physical. I hadn't had to handle that stuff in college, and I was having a difficult time catching the football. It was all very confusing until my second year, but then I hurt my knee and didn't start playing regularly until my third year."

The early failures and frustration drove Biletnikoff to find ways to adapt. Already high-strung, he intensified his efforts to improve, relying on techniques he learned during his senior year in college, when he worked with a former Chicago Bears end named Pete Manning.

"I went back to everything he taught me and just started staying out after practice to work on my footwork," he said. "I couldn't find anything that would make me comfortable and I began to push myself. Then Kenny Stabler came, and it just fit. I just got comfortable and began to concentrate."

Biletnikoff's breakout year was 1967, when he caught 40 passes for 876 yards and five touchdowns. For the next nine seasons, he would catch 40 or more passes, leading the league in 1971 with 61 catches. He was all-AFL in 1967 and 1969, and he played in four consecutive NFL All-Pro games, from 1971 to 1974. During his 14-year career, the Raiders compiled a 144–45–9 record as he averaged 15.2 yards a catch.

Yet there is not a single moment on the field that stands out for Biletnikoff, not even the 1977 Super Bowl, when as the game's Most Valuable Player he caught four passes for 79 yards.

"There really isn't a game that I could pick out," he said, and when pressed, he didn't even point to the Super Bowl. Instead it was the legendary "Sea of Hands Game" on December 21, 1974, against the Miami Dolphins, when he snared two last-minute catches for consecutive first downs. A few plays later, the Raiders scored the game-winning touchdown.

"Those were tough catches to help get us a touchdown at the end of the game," he said.

As the Raiders peaked with the 1977 Super Bowl win, so, too, did Biletnikoff.

"It was just a good mix of guys," he said. "Just football players, that was the whole thing. There was a great deal of peer pressure to work and perform well, and we worked well together as a unit. John [Madden] was a good guy, and he never tried to tie anyone's hands. You just took care of your job and that's all there was."

The season after the Raiders won the Super Bowl, Biletnikoff caught just 33 passes, the first time in a decade he didn't have at least 40 completions. In 1978, his declining skills were becoming obvious. He caught just 20 passes, and it was clear that his career was coming to an end. He was cut loose by the Raiders after the 1978 season, ending one of the most productive careers of any NFL receiver.

After spending so much time in the NFL, Biletnikoff, at age 36, was forced to consider what the rest of his life would be like without football.

It didn't take long for him to get back in the game, this time in the Canadian Football League.

After a year at home, he joined the Montreal Alouettes, partly out of his desire to play again and partly to help out Joe Scannella, a special team coach with the Raiders in 1977, who was then the Alouettes head coach.

Then he returned to southern California and began a coaching career. Unlike other former players who move into the professional coaching ranks after finishing their careers, Biletnikoff began at the bottom, first at the high school level, then moving up to junior college. In time, he coached for two different teams in the USFL and in the Canadian Football League with the Calgary Stampede.

Early on, he demanded the same level of perfection from his players as he did from himself when he played.

"When I first started to coach, I was intense," he said. "That intensity was good to deal with myself, but as a coach you're dealing with a bunch of different personalities. You can't shape guys into what you were like, so I've mellowed. When we played together years ago, you did the extra work on your own and you had to work your ass off, because there was nowhere else to go. But now everything is scheduled for the players, and there are very few that go past what's expected."

As Biletnikoff paid his coaching dues, his NFL career did not fade from memory. In July 1988, he was inducted into the NFL Hall of Fame, reaching the ultimate NFL achievement.

"As a player, I never thought about the Hall of Fame, but it's important to me," he said. "But when you're coaching, there is limited free time, and I've only been [to Canton] when I was inducted. I want the opportunity to go back. I miss the camaraderie among the guys you used to play against."

Then, in 1989, Biletnikoff came full circle when he rejoined the Raiders as the wide receivers coach.

Today, he still handles the receivers for the Raiders, a job that allows him to stay connected to the NFL—but time and tragedy have reshaped his view of football.

In 1992, he beat prostate cancer, with the doctors successfully removing cancerous growths just five months after his third wife, Angela, gave birth to a daughter, Dacia.

It was a sobering experience for him, injecting some perspective into the win-at-all-costs mind-set of the NFL.

In February 1998, Biletnikoff suffered a parent's worst nightmare. His 20-year-old daughter, Tracey, was found strangled to death, allegedly by her former boyfriend.

Tracey was the third of Biletnikoff's five children, and she had overcome drug problems that led her through two stints of rehabilitation. She was on her way to beating the problem when the police found her, then knocked on her father's door in the middle of the night.

"It took me a year to come back with the fact of working through that every day," Biletnikoff said. "I look back in 1992 when I had prostate cancer and I beat that. With this, it is just so tough to understand. You always think that these types of things happen to someone else, as ugly as it seems. But it is an ugly part of life that happens, and it happened to us. That's the way we have to handle it."

Biletnikoff and his wife have created a foundation in Tracey's name to help fund domestic-violence programs, and while he remains committed to coaching, the thought of his slain daughter can obviously diminish the pressures of NFL football.

"I like coaching a lot, but it's tough to coach and not feel that at some point there is more," he said. "You try to be as intense as you can, but with the death of my daughter, you realize there is more to life."

Frederick (Fred) Biletnikoff

Born February 23, 1943, at Erie, PA
Height: 6'1" Weight: 190
High School: Erie, PA, Technical Memorial.
Attended Florida State University.

Brother of Bob Biletnikoff, former outfielder in New York Yankees organization.
Named to *The Sporting News* AFL All-Star Team, 1969.
Named to *The Sporting News* AFC All-Star Team, 1972 and 1973.
Selected by Oakland in 2nd round of 1965 AFL draft.

Year	Club	PASS RECEIVING					TOTAL		
		G.	P.C.	Yds.	Avg.	TD	TD	Pts.	F.
1965	Oakland AFL	14	24	331	13.8	0	0	0	0
1966	Oakland AFL	10	17	272	16.0	3	3	18	2
1967	Oakland AFL	14	40	876	21.9	5	5	30	1
1968	Oakland AFL	14	61	1037	17.0	6	7	42	0
1969	Oakland AFL	14	54	837	15.5	12	12	72	1
1970	Oakland NFL	14	45	768	17.1	7	7	42	0
1971	Oakland NFL	14	*61	929	15.2	9	9	54	1
1972	Oakland NFL	14	58	802	13.8	7	7	42	0
1973	Oakland NFL	14	48	660	13.8	4	4	24	0
1974	Oakland NFL	14	42	593	14.1	7	7	42	0
1975	Oakland NFL	11	43	587	13.7	2	2	12	0
1976	Oakland NFL	13	43	551	12.8	7	7	42	0
1977	Oakland NFL	14	33	446	13.5	5	5	30	1
1978	Oakland NFL	16	20	285	14.3	2	2	12	0
Pro Totals—14 Years		190	589	8974	15.2	76	77	462	6

Additional pro statistics: Scored touchdown on seven-yard fumble recovery run, 1968.
  Played in AFL All-Star Game following 1967 and 1969 seasons.
  Played in Pro Bowl following 1971 through 1974 seasons.
  Played in AFL Championship Game, 1967 through 1969.
  Played in AFC Championship Game following 1970, 1973, 1974, 1976, and 1977 seasons.
  Played in AFL-NFL Championship Game following 1967 season.
  Played in NFL Championship Game following 1976 season.

RESOURCES

Bradley, John Ed. "A Block at Tackle," *Sports Illustrated*, September 5, 1994.

Braucher, Bill. "Looms the Mad Stork," *Sport*, July 1972.

Chamberlin, David. "John Madden, Mr. Big," *Los Angeles Times Magazine*, January 25, 1987.

Deford, Frank. "The Guard Who Would Be Quarterback," *Sports Illustrated*, September 14, 1987.

Dickey, Glenn. "Biletnikoff, Brown Step Out of the Past," *San Francisco Chronicle*, August 6, 1977.

George, Thomas. "Once Just a Union Man, He Is Now a Major Player," *New York Times*, August 11, 1996.

Nack, William. "Thrown for Heavy Losses," *Sports Illustrated*, March 24, 1986.

Ribowsky, Mark. *Slick: The Silver and Black Life of Al Davis*. New York: Macmillan, 1998.

Robertson, Linda. "Pride & Poison," *Miami Herald*, June 24, 1990.

Simmons, Ira. *Black Knight: Al Davis and His Raiders*. Rocklin, California: Prima Publishing, 1990.

Soliday, Bill. "Obsessed with Winning, Dogged by Controversy," *The Oakland Tribune*, December 29, 1999.

Stabler, Ken. *Snake*. New York: Doubleday, 1986.

Tatum, Jack. *They Call Me Assassin*. New York: Everest House, 1979.

INDEX

Page numbers in italics indicate photographs